I0155191

A CASE OF
FOUR PILLOWS

A Play

Gbanabom Hallowell

Sierra Leonean Writers Series

A Case of Four Pillows

ISBN: 978-9988-8743-4-6

Sierra Leonean Writers Series

120 Kissy Road, Freetown, Sierra Leone
Kofi Annan Avenue, North Legon, Accra, Ghana
Publisher: Prof. Osman Sankoh (Mallam O.)
publisher@sl-writers-series.org
www.sl-writers-series.org

"At the touch of love everyone becomes a poet"
—Plato

"Any woman, who is sure of her own wits, is a match, at any time, for a man who is not sure of his own temper."
—Wilkie Collins

Books by Gbanabom Hallowell

POEMS

Hills of Temper (1996)
Drumbeats of War (2004)
My Immigrant Blood (2006)
Manscape in the Sierra: New & Collected Poems 1991-2011 (SLWS, 2012)
A Little After Dawn (2013)
When Sierra Leone Was a Woman (2014)
Don't Call Me Elvis and Other Poems (SLWS, 2016)
The Art of the Lonely Wanderer (SLWS, 2016)
Anatomy of Love (SLWS, 2017)

EDITED BOOKS

Leoneanthology: Contemporary Short Stories & Poems from Sierra Leone (SLWS, 2016)
In the Belly of the Lion: An Anthology of New Sierra Leonean Short Stories (SLWS, 2015)

FICTION

Gbomgbosoro: Two Short Stories (SLWS, 2012)
The Road to Kaibara (SLWS, 2016)

WAR DIARY

Tears of the Sweet Peninsula: May 25, 1997 and the Sierra Leone Civil Conflict (2005)

PLAYS

A Case of Four Pillows (SLWS, 2017)

ACKNOWLEDGMENTS

Although I'd written a few literary works, I needed help with *A Case of Four Pillows* as it was my premier attempt at writing a stage play. Stage plays and screenplays necessitate adequate attention to the craft's technical requirements. Colleagues of mine allowed me to benefit from their practitioner expertise and professionalism.

The play is largely written in English and partially in Krio. With regards to the Krio in the play, I needed a native speaker, who was also literate in the standard Krio orthography, to transcribe the texts. For that, I thank Mrs. Sophie Allieu, nee Amadu-Taylor, a writer and consultant, who transcribed the script from my sub-standard Krio to that of the nationally recognized orthography.

Mrs. Elizabeth Lucy Kamara, Head of the English Unit in the Department of Language Studies, Fourah Bay College, University of Sierra Leone, did a commendable work in copyediting the entire script and in convincing me that it was important that the Krio Language in the play be written in the recognized orthography. I thank her profusely.

Thanks also go to Mr. Thomas P. Sowa, Director of Administration and Human resources of Sierra Leone Broadcasting Corporation (SLBC) for copyediting a few sections in the play.

Mr. Abdulai Walon-Jalloh, a poet and playwright, and a lecturer of Linguistics, Department of Language Studies, Fourah Bay College, University of Sierra Leone, submitted the initial preview of the play with valuable recommendations that fired my imagination to stretch the play beyond a closure other than what it originally was. I thank him for that.

The play is coming out at a time the Sierra Leone theatre had long been abandoned by the viewing public, and, because of adverse conditions, neglected by its leading practitioners. Young practitioners of the performing art are today utterly attracted to the movie industry at the expense of the solitary stage. At the time of writing, I was constantly tempted by some of these young artists, to convert the then unfinished manuscript from a stage play to a screen movie; but as I have stated above, I was mindful of the challenges a departure from stage to screen would have posed to a writer only venturing into the genre.

I thought I had to be allowed to begin with the traditional stage play before branching out to any literary daiquiri of play writing. I explained to my younger friends that I would have to first learn the techniques of screenwriting. And for those friends of mine and all lovers of the art, I sincerely hope that this stage play would be made into a screen movie for the benefit of my friends, if it's worth any effort, by those who have mastered the game.

Certainly, I would be excited to see my play both on stage and on screen; however, I'm thankful to my middle-aged wit that values the power of the traditional theatre stage, and hope that the university lecturer, Philip Yamba Thullah of the Department of Language and Cultural Studies, Njala University who had read and showed interest in having his students stage the play, will succeed in his desire to stage the play on his university campus theatre. I hope he would accept my thanks in advance if he ever succeeded in staging the play.

Of course, needless to say that, as the author, I alone bear the blame for any fault that the play might have in it, on the basis that, regardless of any intervention made, I single-handedly decided what changes to accept or not, and how to include them in the play.

CHARACTERS
(In alphabetical order)

Alhaji Majid	Father of Khadija
Child Falilu	Childhood flashback
Child Fudia	Childhood flashback
Falilu	A handsome 23 year old student
Fudia	A beautiful 21 year old student
Isatu	Khadija's 18 year old cousin
Khadija	An attractive student, age 19
Kongoma	
Kongosa	
Kortu	
Mother	Mother of Khadija/wife of Alhaji
Njai	A handsome 23 year old student
Professor Sankoh	
Saleswoman	
Two officers	
Voice	
Security	
Students	
Teen Falilu	Teenage flashback
Teen Fudia	Teenage flashback
Tigi	A 22 year old college student

A Case of Four Pillows

ACT ONE
SCENE ONE

The scene opens in an empty university classroom. Falilu sits at a desk bowing over a book. In less than ten seconds of silence, Fudia, in a slightly torn dress, hastens through the door and sits at a desk four rows away from Falilu. She cups her face in her hands and sobs. He raises his head and stares at her. He quickly drops his book and dashes over to her.

Falilu:

Fudia! Again?

Tell me it's not what I'm thinking.

She continues to bow, sobbing. He reaches his hand and touches her shoulder.

Look at you, all bleeding.

How can he treat you like this?

He kneels halfway before her.

What! What! Such big bruises!

Fudia:

Bruises! What bruises?

Falilu:

Oh, come off it, Fudia.

Must you hide a killer-skin?

Come with me,

I need to take

You to the campus doctor.

Fudia:

She springs up.

Oh no, o, no, no!

1

You know I dare not go
There looking like this!

Falilu:

Looking like what? You are at it again.
You continue to protect him?
He is just a beast!
Who beats up a girlfriend like this?
Let's be off to see the doctor.

Fudia:

But I'm not sick!

Falilu:

Oh yeah!

Fudia:

He was only just a little drunk.
Maybe I should have
Let him go to bed
Like he insisted;
All I wanted was for us to work
On the assignment, and he would
Have nothing of that…

Falilu:

There you go again,
Defending his actions. Must you
Always be a victim of his violence?
Now look at you…someone's daughter.
How long must you be a victim
Of his drunkenness?

Fudia:

She stares at him for a while.
Don't talk like that!

Don't you see
I was wrong too.
Maybe I went too far.
She pauses a while and changes the subject.
Listen, Falilu, I have lost
My note book where I had
Professor Sankoh's assignment.
I must complete
Our group assignment
Before the professor comes to class.

Falilu:

This is really not the time
For assignments.
You must take care of yourself first,
Sores and torn dress.
You can always....

Fudia:

...don't you patronize me, Falilu.
I probably deserve it...but
I have my college assignments
To think about,
And I must
Muscle up the courage
To do them otherwise...
I may not make the grade.
So thank you
For being my father,
And loan me
Your book to complete
My group's work.

Falilu:

He reluctantly removes a book from his bag and gives it to her.

Someone should teach that fellow

A lesson not to mess up

With someone else's daughter.

Fudia:

Why don't you just stop

Being my father?

I keep telling you always

To stop being my dad.

I can take care of myself!

Falilu:

I bet you can.

Dear God, this is not happening.

Fudia:

She sits at another desk and opens Falilu's book

Eh! I thought we were supposed

To compare metaphysical poetry

In John Donne's days

To contemporary ones?

How come your question is different

From the one I had in my book?

Falilu:

So much for being attentive!

That's an earlier assignment.

We submitted that a long time ago.

The one in question

Is on page seventy-six.

Now you better go

Look for your group
Before Professor Sankoh
Comes in here.

Fudia:

That's what
I was trying to tell you...
I am in the same group as Njai,
And he wouldn't hear me telling him
We needed to wake
Up and work on the assignment.

Falilu:

Well, you had
*B*etter wake up on your own,
With only a few more months
To go through it all...

Fudia:

Grrrrrrrr!

Falilu:

Okay, okay, okay!
Not that I want to be told
That I'm not your father, but
I can see your assignment
Taking a wrong turn.
*The mingling voices of approaching students increase in
volume. She rearranges her dress and wipes her face of the
crust of blood.*

Fudia:

Am I okay, Falilu?

Falilu:

Next time

	It's your skin he will peel off.
Njai:	

Njai dashes in and Tigi, his friend, follows after.
I heard that one, father Falilu.
Hasn't Fudia
Always told you her real
Father is still alive?

Falilu:

As he goes to a back seat:
Are you not man enough
To know that she deserves
To be treated better?

Njai:

Oh yeah?
Your Khadija
Is the luckiest girl
On campus because you treat
Her just like a queen,
Right, Father-Daddy?

Falilu:

He dashes from the back of the class and stops before Njai
Don't you dare mention
Her name in your foul mouth!

Tigi:

Watch it, big daddy!

Njai:

So what, father daddy?
He mimics a panicking voice
Are you going to kill me now?
He utters a big laugh and dashes around the classroom.

Fudia:

> That's enough, Njai.
> Falilu has a right to protect me from any harm!
> *Njai runs up to Fudia and wraps his arms around her.*
> *Grudgingly, Falilu walks off to the back of the class.*
> *Wai!,* you are hurting my arm.
> See where you bruised me
> Against the wall.

Njai

> Hey baby girl,
> I already told you I'm sorry.
> The devil
> In my head was playing
> Tricks with me.

Fudia:

> Just tell me you were drunk
> And couldn't control yourself,
> And now here we are, unable
> To do anything
> Regarding
> Our group assignment.

Njai:

> Don't you worry, my darling,
> Tigi managed to do something
> Before Professor Sankoh's class.

Tigi:

> That's right,
> I managed to put something
> Together for us three,
> My dear Fudia!

Fudia:

But I wanted to be a part
Of the assignment, myself.
How could you do it all on your own?
It's a group work, remember?

Njai:

No queen suffers in my kingdom.
Relax my baby girl.
The work is done and ready
For Professor Sankoh.

Tigi:

Exactly!
You heard your king speaking.
*The noises made by the students surge and increase in volume
outside of the class as footsteps approach. Screaming voices
and screeching of chairs continue for a while then the
classroom door opens and fifteen students rush in to occupy
desks. In the eerie quietness, Professor Sankoh enters.*

Prof. Sankoh:

*He paces excitedly in the quiet classroom. His behavior is
between that of a genius and an erratic professor,*
As serene as the early waters
Of the morning blue sea,
We continue to shower in the studies
Of Metaphysical Poetry.
*He pauses, looks about him, and surveys the students in the
class. The class remains quiet and attentive.*
That's right!
A good crop of honors students
Ready to sink their teeth in the classics...

British literary classics, to be precise…
*He dashes to the Board, writes something on it, and quickly
erases it.*
Like I promised you in our last class,
We are done, looking
At metaphysical poetry
As an invention of John Donne
Or his generation.
If anything,
Metaphysical Poetry
Flourishes in our generation,
Particularly in the African generation,
More than it did in
John Donne's generation.
Today, our concentration
Will be contemporary Metaphysical
Poetry of the romantic.
The class giggles, a long murmuring.
Now, let's have some reaction
To my postulation.
What Sierra Leonean poet
Grapples with
The theories of romantic metaphysics?

Falilu:
He raises a hand.
Yes sir!

Professor Sankoh:
Unnecessary to raise a hand,
Bombard!
The class laughs boisterously.

Falilu:

We can begin to count
Syl Cheney-Coker
Among Africa's
Best Metaphysical
Poets of the romantic.

Njai:

He turns to Falilu.
This is because you have not
Seen enough of his anger
As a protest poet, always
Searching for his identity
In his Afro-Saxon heritage.

Falilu

He turns to Njai.
Some of us have a keen eye
And can see when
Poets and students
Of poetry are capable of loving...

Fudia:

Falilu, stop!

Njai:

Let him be, please.
He turns to Professor Sankoh.
With your permission Professor,
May I ask Falilu to point
To the romantic in Cheney-Coker's
Literary career?

Prof. Sankoh:

Yes, you may.

And I do hope
He will back his argument
With a sound
Theoretic understanding?
Njai and the rest of the class stare at Falilu.

Falilu:

He walks to the top of the class.
What better Cheney-Coker poem
To remind you of than
"Poem for a Lost Lover?"

Prof. Sankoh:

That indeed is a good example
Of Cheney-Coker as a Metaphysical poet
Of the romantic.

Falilu:

"Eyes of heavenly essence, O breasts of the purity of breasts
Russian sapphire of the blue of eyes
O wine that mellows like the plenitude of Bach
Sargassian sea that is the calm of your heart
the patience of you loving my fragile soul
the courage of you moulding my moody words
I love you woman gentle in my memory!"

Professor Sankoh:

What a beautiful rendition
Of modern poetic lines
From a metaphysical
Poet of the romantic.
Now, Falilu
Expatiate on the relevance
Of your reading!

Falilu:

I identify with
The poet as well as the persona...
The honest whisper of losing
A woman of substance...
The catharsis of the poet's pain,
And I wish every person
In my generation can
Appreciate and dignify love.

Njai:

He rises from his seat and speaks to Professor Sankoh
I hold a lenient view
Regarding the interpretation
Given by Falilu
To the stanza he just read.
I sense deceit underneath
The mourning coming from
The persona in the lines...the sense
Of unrequited love abounds.

Falilu:

He rises from his seat and speaks to Njai
Could you substantiate your claim
Of unrequited love
With evidence drawn
From the lines I just read?

Njai:

That's exactly what I am driving at,
That by your choice of which
Verse to read from the poem,
And backed by

Your emotional reaction to that reading,
You present the persona
In your own thoughts
And not in the thought of the poem.

Falilu:

I could read you
The second and third
Stanzas, and you would not be able
To see the feel in the eyes of love.
For a starter,
I do hope you agree that the persona
Is lamenting after losing a loved one.
Njai, have you lost a loved one before?
And do you have
The attributes to express
The reason for that?
He pauses a while then continues.
My hope here is that you do have emotions
And that you do love?
If you do, allow the following lines
To appeal to all your human senses
And I quote again:
"the patience of you loving my fragile soul
the courage of you moulding my moody words
I love you woman gentle in my memory!"

Njai:

Your quoted words
Even in repeating them,
Do not open any room to debunk
My observation of the absence

Of unrequited love.
I fail to see
The romantic nature of the love.
I'd rather wait until
The entire poems is presented
If I must read it to make sense to my peers.
I rest my case, Professor Sankoh.
Professor Sankoh springs up but says nothing. He paces back and forth and stands still.

Falilu:

In the affairs of love,
One is required to have a fragile soul
For a lovely woman, otherwise
One would be unable
To experience
Any gentle memory of her.
Have you ever had a fragile soul
For a woman you love?

Professor Sankoh:

What do our ladies
Think about the stanzas
And the debate between
Falilu and Njai?

Khadija:

She rises from her seat
I would say that if I was hiding
In a corner, and my lover
Was lamenting in the lines
Of the poem as
I heard from Falilu,

I would be moved to tears.
She sits.

Fudia:

She rises from her seat
I would agree with Njai that it takes
More than a stanza from a poem
Of three or more verses
To determine the integrity of a persona.
We should bear in mind that
The mood of the persona could change
From line to line or from stanza to stanza.
Even the stanza
We listened to has the persona
Confessing to having moody words.
Njai's argument synchronizes
With mine that love could
Be as moody as the words
That express them.
She sits.

Prof. Sankoh:

Now the tone has been set
For our concluding classes
In the coming months.
He goes to the chalkboard.
The assignment for this class
Is for each of you to go and
Research two African Metaphysical Poets
Of the romantic, and develop
A comparative analysis of their treatment
Of the themes of love for country,

Partner and virtue.
Drop off your last assignments
In the drop off box as you go outside.
Class dismissed.

Professor Sankoh quickly gathers his belongings and commends the class. The entire class rises and applauds. As they exit the door, Njai steps aside from the other students and bursts out laughing. The students pause in their movements. Njai turns to Falilu:

Njai:

I'm sure you realized
You couldn't make the argument.
Even Fudia agreed with my analysis
On the basis of its strength.
Want more proof of my strength
On the subject, right now?

Falilu:

Oh yeah?
And you are suddenly a peacock?
Well you think about this right now:
"I would challenge you to a battle of wits,
But I see you are unharmed."

D   *He leaves the scene.*

Students:

Shout a chorus and applauding.
Shakespeare, Shakespeare
Shakespeare, Shakespeare
Shakespeare, Shakespeare

THE CURTAINS FALL

ACT ONE
SCENE TWO

The scene opens to a sizeable garden where students usually sit to relax and to read or just converse. At present, enter Khadija covered in 'hijab', and Fudia in jeans. They both occupy a long bench, sitting opposite of each other.

Khadija:

Falilu has asked me to marry him
After honors class.

Fudia:

Excitedly.
Did he?
What did you tell him?

Khadija:

I told him
I didn't know what to say.

Fudia:

How could you say a thing like that?
You two have been together
Since first year?
Four years later you still don't
Know what to say?

Khadija:

Fudia, you know me now.
I have told you how my parents
Would react if I was to ever tell them
About Falilu's Christian background.

Fudia:

But you have to maintain

Your stand because you love him…
And you will not settle
For any other man,
Muslim or otherwise.

Khadija:

She shakes her head.
You won't understand.

Fudia:

There is nothing to understand.
Falilu is a good man.
Don't let him go.

Khadija:

I know Falilu is indeed a good man,
And over the period of four years
He has been nothing
But a good lover to me.
She pauses, and then takes Fudia's hand.
I wish my parents
Would have that picture
Of him in their hearts.

Fudia:

What matters is that you have
That picture of the man
Who wants to ask for your hand.

Khadija:

They won't hate him as a person,
But if you understand what *our* religion
Means to my parents,
You will understand
The things I am going through.

She releases Fudia's hand.

Fudia:

Khadija, is there anything
I can do to help
Soften your parents?
I have never met them before,
But if you oblige *some more*
Pertinent information
To me, I can try...

Khadija:

Don't even try it, please.

Fudia:

But I will...

Khadija:

You will? You will what?
There is nothing you can do
To change my parents' mind.
She pauses in steps and in speech.
Look, I love Falilu, and
I hope that things
Work between us...

Fudia:

What, Khadija?
...anything wrong between
You and Falilu?
Anything I do not know?

Khadija:

There is nothing happening other
Than that my parents are stressing
My life about who and when to marry.

They won't accept Falilu
In a hundred years
And they won't leave me alone
To pursue my education.
They are planning to marry me
Off just after college.

Fudia:

Shocked, she moves closer to Khadija.
This is not good.
Why did they allow you to come
To college in the first place?

Khadija:

They never allowed me.
They never wanted
Me to go to school.
I only found out this semester
That the man
They intend to marry me
Off to has been
Paying my fees in college.
I don't even know him....
I'm told he is almost my father's age.

Fudia:

What? Does Falilu know about this?

Khadija:

No.

Fudia:

Are you not going to tell him?

Khadija:

No!

        I don't intend telling him just yet,
        Because he wouldn't understand.

Fudia:

        If you tell him now, you could
        Both decide what to do about it.

Khadija:

        I am not going to tell him
        Because it will not happen.

Fudia:

        She giggles.
        How do you mean?

Khadija:

        I intend to fail my course this year,
        So I will have another year
        To repeat the class...
        And everything else would have to wait
        Until I finish college.

Fudia:

        What are you saying?

Khadija:

        My hope is that Falilu would
        Have graduated;
        Found a job...an easy enough reason
        For me to elope with him to wherever...
        As long as my parents cannot
        Reach me until they come to their senses.

Fudia:

        I'm glad you love my friend
        That much
        But don't you think that action

You contemplate
Is too extreme?

Khadija:

Promise me you will not tell him
My plan or say anything about it to him.

Fudia:

You have my word.
However, I sincerely hope
The relationship will work
Out for you and Falilu
Without you having to unnecessarily
Repeat a class.

Khadija:

I could be a good lawyer
But my father wouldn't hear about it.
Oh dear, Fudia,
I must be on my way.
It's time for prayer.
I better hurry fast,
Members of the Jamaat
Would be asking after me.
Please extend my regards to Falilu.
He knows I love him so I will not
Ask you to blow a kiss for me.

She hurries away from the scene and disappears. Fudia continues to take pebbles and throw them away from her, deeply lost in thought. Falilu enters the scene as he hurries, walking by undecidedly.

Fudia:

Hey Falilu!

Falilu:

He stops instantly.

What are you doing here all alone?

Fudia:

What are *you* doing here?

Falilu:

He walks over to Fudia.

Have you seen Khadija?

Fudia:

Mmmmmmm lover boy!

Falilu:

It's not like that.

Fudia:

It's like what now?

Falilu:

Fudia

He breathes hard.

Khadija is killing my dreams.

Fudia:

Why would you say a thing

Like that about a woman

Who loves you so much?

Falilu:

Almost screams.

And yet couldn't take me

To meet her parents?

He pauses a while then catches his breath.

I have asked her to accept my proposal

So that we get married

Right after college.

I'm just frustrated
I don't know what to do.
She probably
Has another lover
Outside of this university.
All I want is for her to tell me
That and I will leave her alone.

Fudia:

She stands up and approaches Falilu.
Don't you think you are just
Speaking out your fears?
When did you tell her that you wish
To marry her?

Falilu:

It's been a week now,
And ever since we discussed that
She has been dodging me.
I don't see her as often as before.
Can't concentrate on my work
And we have
Our finals coming soon.

Fudia:

Tell her again; matter of fact,
Show it to her
That you wish to marry her...

Falilu:

But I already did...

Fudia:

Ten times over...
Tell her ten times over.

Tell her every day, every hour,
Every minute…

Falilu:

Stop, stop that…

Fudia:

I know you love Khadija,
But it's dangerous to try to read
Too much into why you are not
Seeing much of her.
Call her on her phone.
Once is not enough!
Talk to her seventy times seven times.

Falilu:

Frustratingly.

She won't even pick up her phone!
I have called her line a dozen times
In the last five minutes.
All I hear is her voice,
"leave me a message and I will call you back."
I have left her many *many* messages,
And she has not called back.
Hellooooo!
Do you see now what I mean?
Do you see it *now?*

Fudia:

Hesitantly.
It's not like Khadija to do such a thing.
Something has to be the problem.

Falilu:

Yeah, something is the problem,

Like having another boyfriend
Taking her attention!
He pauses and giggles. His phone rings. They both pause.
Oh well, there is always
Someone else who will love you
If no one else does. Excuse me Fudia.
He picks the call and moves a little away.

Fudia:

She shouts at Falilu.
Don't do that Falilu.
You two have nurtured this love
For four years;
Don't push it down the drain.
Falilu continues to chat with the caller on his phone. Occasionally he laughs to himself. He continues like that until he edges off the scene.

THE CURTAINS FALL

ACT ONE
SCENE THREE

*The scene is at the students' canteen and about fifteen
students, male and female, sit in groups, eating and drinking
and chatting. Two waiters and waitresses spill around the
student customers. Some students are visibly drunk but they
remain relatively calm although they continue to chatter. A
somber music plays for a while before fading out.*

Tigi:

He staggers around the table with a bottle in hand.
All three of them have felt me.
All three of them have been my girls
Since they entered college.
They received a good piece of me.
They used to say,
"You are great, man!"

Njai:

You know I'm the king.
I don't like piling girls around me.
I like them one at a time.
They nag when
you crowd yourself with them.
They nag with problems and requests.

Kortu:

He speaks behind the back of Njai.
Njai, you talk too much.
How about
Just trying to shut up
Or keeping it low.

Who cares about
Your prowess?

Njai:

He turns around to the table where the voice comes from.
Who was that who spoke
To me and about me?
Nobody owns up
Good-for-nothing students are you?

Tigi

He joins Njai.
Oh, a bunch of Grade C students!
Njai and Tigi move around the table of the other guests and stopping at Kortu's.
You see, as seniors who have worked
Very hard to be at the honors roll,
Today we look back at our toiling.

Kortu:

We don't want any trouble.
We are just here to enjoy the weekend,
And that's all. Why don't you guys
Go back to your table
And continue your fun?

Tigi:

And what's your name?

Kortu:

That isn't really necessary,
But if you must ask, its Brima here,
Victor there and I'm Kortu.

Njai:

Kortu, I have had many more girls

On campus than you will ever
Dream of having.
So, next time when
Any of my friends or I'm reminiscing,
Please stay out of it or beg me
To teach you how to be *a* man.

Tigi:

He sings:
"I'm the man, I'm the man,
I'm the man, and I'm the man!
You have to tell everybody
That I'm the man, I'm the man, I'm the man!"
(Song by Aloe Blacc)

Njai:

He walks up to Kortu and hooks his chin with his forefinger.
I think that as a freshman in college
You should regard your seniors.
At this point Fudia enters but seeing the altercation, she begins to back off.
Fudia, come right in, my dear.
This freshman fellow called Kortu—
We're just getting to know each other.
I finally met him.
The new college smart kid,
Whom I'm told has a crush on you.
Or is he one of the numbers
Of boyfriends you would be dating
After me?

Fudia:

Stop this nonsense, Njai.

See how you are embarrassing yourself.

Can't you be decent for once?

Tigi:

But Fudia, you just have to deny

Or accept that Kortu is interfering

In my friend's garden.

Kortu then slaps Njai's finger from his face. Njai and Kortu throw jabs at each other as Kortu's friends join in on the one side and Tigi's on the other. The other students who are minding their businesses come to the rescue to stop the fight. After they are parted, Njai turns to the direction of Fudia who continues to stir at him.

Fudia:

You are a pathetic man.

It's all over between us.

She begins to walk to the door.

Njai:

He chases Fudia.

Don't you dare walk away from me,

Fudia. You caused this problem.

If you had kept your legs together

Like a decent woman

Nothing like this would have happened.

Fudia:

Tell that to your sisters not me!

You are just an idiot!

Njai chases Fudia out of the door. Tigi runs out following both of them. The scene moves on to Falilu's room, where he is busy studying under a table lamp. After a while, his door is knocked on. He inquires who it is but nobody answers.

*He goes to the door and opens it and in dashes Fudia,
sobbing; her clothes all torn. She falls in Falilu's bed still
sobbing.*

Falilu:

It's Njai again?
*Fudia keeps sobbing. He goes out of his room in a rush to
look for who else is there. He shouts at the dark distance.*
Njai! Njai!
I know you are standing
Somewhere in the dark
Listening to me.
How can you say you love a woman
And you are always hurting her?
If you think she is not good for you
Why don't you spare yourself the effort
And not subdue her to violence?
He pauses.
You should be lucky
I have to accommodate
You because
Fudia returns your love.
Why don't you be a man and leave
Her alone and go after another girl?
*From the bulrushes in the dark in front of Falilu's
apartment enters Njai followed by Tigi. Tigi steps ahead of
Njai and approaches Falilu.*

Tigi:

Falilu, we are not here for trouble.
Njai is very sorry for what happened
At the canteen tonight.

Falilu:

And what exactly happened that
Fudia should come running
To me in a torn dress?

Tigi:

It was just a small misunderstanding....
Listen, I know if Njai has access
To Fudia now,
They will solve it in no time.

Njai:

Speaking to Falilu.
Hey man, I know you care about
Protecting Fudia from harm,
But not from me.

Falilu:

But you have harmed her quite
A lot since you two began dating
Only in the final year.

Njai:

How can you talk like that, Falilu?
You know how Fudia's past lovers
On this campus treated her.
I have stayed the longest with her,
What doesn't that tell you?
I have been good to her.

Falilu:

Is stripping her naked in public
And making her to bleed from
Her head down
What you call being good

To her?
You are a piece of shit.

Njai:

Njai advances angrily to face Falilu but is restrained by Tigi.
Hey!
Hold your tongue on me
Okay? Otherwise...

Falilu:

...otherwise what?
Njai, you better just leave.
You don't deserve this lady.
I will not allow you
To see her tonight.
Is it not enough that you have
Succeeded in embarrassing her?
You're violent to those who love
You and want to be with you.
I wish you allow Fudia
To be the person
She wants to be with you...

Njai:

Did she tell you she
Doesn't want me anymore?

Falilu:

It's not for me to say, but how
I wish she could arrive
At that conclusion.
Go to your hostel and spend
Some time
To think over your actions tonight,

And decide like a boy
Who wants to grow into a man.

Njai:

Are you suggesting that
I apologize to her?
It's best now
If that's what you want.

Tigi:

To Falilu.
Hey man, Falilu,
I believe that
With your intervention
You can help to settle
This misunderstanding
Tonight, once and for all.
Just allow Njai to see her
And say he's sorry.
I think that will help.

Falilu:

Thinks for a while.
Listen, Tigi,
I will tell her you guys
Want to say sorry but it's up to her
To decide her action.
However, let me ask you,
Njai, what do you want from Fudia?

Njai:

He gyrates frustratingly.
How can you ask me that question?
I love her, and that's it.

Would you just allow me to see her?
I need to talk to my girl.

Falilu:

Do you know what love is?

Njai:

This is getting serious.
What!!
Do you want
To be the good Professor
And run Cheney-Coker
Down my throat
Just because you
Read the wrong stanza
From his "Poem to My Lost Lover?"
Are you now deciding whom Fudia
Should call a lost lover? I am not
A lost lover, you know that.
I am a lover in lust.
He bursts out laughing.
I don't believe this shit.
You making me
See Fudia or not?

Falilu:

It's up to her, not me.
He returns to his hostel door and slams it behind him.

Tigi:

Just take it easy, Njai.
It will all be good.

Njai:

Don't tell me that.

You should know
I'm doing Fudia a favor.

Tigi:

I know.

Falilu's hostel door opens and he walks out alone.

Falilu:

Sorry, she is not
Ready to see you, not tonight.

Njai:

You are responsible for this,
Mr. Father Daddy.
Go to hell, you'll see she will
Come back to me tomorrow.
As he and Tigi walk away.
You are nothing
But a bookworm bully,
Mr. Father Daddy.

Falilu:

And you are a bedroom bully!
Falilu returns to his room. Fudia rises from the bed and approaches Falilu.

Fudia:

Has he gone away?

Falilu:

Yeah, he has gone away.
He sits at his study desk gazing at his book.

Fudia:

Sorry, Falilu
For putting you
Through my mess.

Falilu:

What are you talking about?
You didn't cause anyone any mess,
Not Njai, not any of your
Previous boyfriends,
And certainly not yourself!

Fudia:

Previous boyfriends!

Falilu:

I mean your past
Relationships on campus.

Fudia:

Oh wow!
It has come to this, right?
Fudia stares at Falilu guiltily but embarrassingly and angrily.

Falilu:

Listen, I'm sorry, I…
I…I didn't mean it that way…

Fudia:

That's okay Falilu.
She giggles dryly.
I'm working on myself.
After a while
Oh, I need to go to bed.

Falilu:

Yeah, *urrm,*
I will walk you to your hostel.

Fudia:

I'm fine, I'm fine, Falilu;

        I will walk myself. Thanks.

Falilu:

        Are you sure?

        Fudia stares at Falilu for a while nods and disappears from the scene. Falilu bows his head at his desk.

THE CURTAIN FALLS

ACT ONE
SCENE FOUR

The scene opens to a quiet and settled classroom. Professor Sankoh returns from the blackboard after writing "Contemporary Metaphysical Poetry: The African Experience." In his usual exuberance, he paces the front of the room and clears his throat in one long groan.

Prof. Sankoh:

> In our last class, the assignment
> Was for you to research at least
> Two contemporary African
> Metaphysical poets
> Of the romantic, and develop
> A comparative analysis of their treatments
> Of the themes of love for country,
> Partner and for virtue.
> *He paces the aisles of the class making sure the groups are ready to present. He shouts.*
> Group Four! It's your turn.
> *Class waits, no one moves.*
> Who are the students
> Who make up group Four!

Fudia:

> Professor Sankoh
> I am the leader of Group Four
> And we are ready
> To present our assignment.
> *Fudia walks to the front of the class, stands before the class. Professor Sankoh walks to the back. Then Njai rises and*

*walks to the front and stands away from Fudia. Tigi follows
and stands between Fudia and Njai.*
Our group scanned the gamut
Of poets writing in Africa.
We combed collections and anthologies
Of poems from Morocco
To the heartland of South Africa.
We concentrated on poetry written
Or translated into English from
Whatever language, as long as
It was available to us in English.
*She pauses, looks in the direction of both Tigi and Njai, and
receives a nod.*
We were particularly fascinated
By the South African poet,
Dennis Brutus, whom we agreed,
By his use of *conceit* in many
Of his poems show evidence,
As he himself acknowledged,
Of influence from the father
Of 17th century metaphysical poetry,
John Donne.
She retreats.

Njai:

He surges.
And so we concentrated on his
Most famous collection of poems,
Letters to Martha.
After keen studies,
We decided that Dennis Brutus,

In a metaphysical sense,
Shares a major characteristic
With Syl Cheney-Coker:
They both express in their poetry
Love for country
And love for womanhood.
The other day this class identified
Cheney-Coker's "Poem to a Lost Lover"
As an appropriate example
Of his metaphysical standing.
He retreats.

Fudia:

She surges.
In the poem
"A Troubadour," Dennis Brutus,
In comparing his love for his country
And that for his women,
Quoting Isaac I. Elimimian,
Confesses that "He needs the love
Of womanhood
In order to fulfill his destiny."
I found that aspect disparaging
To say the least.
She retreats.

Tigi:

He surges.
But we were quick to correct
A misconception amongst us as researched...

Professor Sankoh:

Excuse me Tigi! Excuse me!

The professor almost dances his way to the front of the class.
I cannot help but stop you there Tigi
To hold Fudia to her observation.
Fudia why are you disparaged
By Professor Elimimian's
Quotation you just rendered?

Fudia:

Thank you Professor Sankoh.
I repeat,
The quotation of Professor Elimimian.
Elimimian noted that Denis Brutus
In his poems manifests that and I quote
"He needs the love
Of womanhood
In order to fulfill his destiny."
It's obviously disgusting that Brutus
Should treat a woman's love as a means
To other ends.
He definitely comes across as a user
And a spoiler.
I rest my case, Professor Sankoh.

Proffesor Sankoh:

Thank you Fudia.
Please continue, Tigi.

Tigi:

He surges.
My research hopes to correct
The misconception critics like Fudia
Have about the legendary poet,
Denis Brutus.

We cautioned that the assertion
Of a single critic
Should not be enough
To sway our opinion of a work
Of art, such as poetry.
We decided
To take the criticism
On a face value…
Not until
I found the following
Line from one of his poems
That reads, "no mistress-favour
Has adorned my breast,"
Which clearly shows that
Denis Brutus is not shown
As a user of women, or that
He engages in romantic love
As a means to other ends.
He retreats.

Njai:

He surges.
Exactly Tigi.
It should be remembered
That apartheid
Was heavy upon the brows
Of writers like Dennis Brutus.
He lived under its pangs,
Which made
Him only a shadow of himself.
He retreats.

Fudia:

> *She surges.*
> I am aware, from the lectures
> Of Professor Sankoh, that
> There is something
> Called "poetic license."
> Who owns that license, if I may ask?
> Is it the poet,
> The poem or the persona?
> In this presentation
> Which are we looking at, Njai?
> *She pauses.*

Njai:

> The license I guess protects
> The three categories
> You have mentioned.

Fudia:

> If you are not as specific
> As my question is, allow me
> To look
> At the poem from the position
> Of the persona because as a woman,
> I have been on the receiving end
> Of this patriarchal society
> And God help
> Me or all the women in this class.
> The world outside there
> Is not the university
> But the multiversity where
> Patriarchal chauvinism has long

Perfected in multiplicity.
As a woman,
I believe that the victim
Is the owner of the license!
I rest my case.

*At the end of their presentation they bow. There emerges
uproar of support with thunderous applause.*

Prof. Sankoh

Thank you for a succinct
But detailed literary appreciation.
Class, you will notice that
The group allowed everyone to stand up
And react independently, and yes,
Subjectively, to the research they did.
Do not be fooled,
Literature matters most
When the subjective is allowed to lead
The analysis.
The only thing you must watch
For is whether the presenter
Has mastered
The content of his or her
Research.
Now I will allow the class
To react to the presentation.
The floor is open.
Just show your hand to speak.

Falilu:

I sense independence of ideas
In the presentation.

What strikes me most
Was the presentation of the clash
Of opinions.
While Fudia based her presentation
On a feminine platform,
The gentlemen
Looked at Dennis Brutus
Against the inhuman apartheid
That consumed South Africa.
Bear in mind that
Brutus was a white poet.
One expected him to be laidback...
But all his life, and in his work
He endured the suffering of the blacks
In his white skin.
I applaud the brutal examination.
I applaud Brutus' duality.

Khadija:

I think that
The duality Falilu speaks
Of in Brutus' work
Compares to the duality
In Cheney-Coker's.
Cheney-Coker writes between
The torments of his
Anglo-Saxon identity.
His poem "Caliban"
Brings out that identity
Clearly and it is one of his
Most metaphysical voices.

Prof. Sankoh:
      Khadija,
      It's interesting you mention
      Cheney-Coker's "Caliban,"
      In which the persona,
      Caliban, laments the two cultures
      Of Africa and Europe between
      Which he feels
      Dangerously suspended;
      Also remember that Fudia
      Was unsympathetic to Brutus,
      Taking him to task for his reckless
      Desire for womanhood.
      Do you believe,
      In trying to respond to Fudia,
      That it is the poet or the persona
      That has the poetic license,
      Or is it the poem
      And how does that help
      To resolve any short sight
      Fudia might have?
      There follows another uproar; the class divides in their responses as they clamor to be heard.
      I meant that question
      As an assignment.
      In our next class, we will listen
      To the final groups of presenters
      Before you all begin to work on
      Your dissertations.
      Class dismissed.

The class leaves the scene. The scene moves to where Tigi and three students enter from the right and on the left enter Kortu and three other students.

Kortu:

I am in search of your friend
To settle scores for my name
And for the name of a decent lady.

Tigi:

My friend, Njai does not settle scores
With a freshman like you.
Why are you cheeky for your class?
You should be nothing
But a humble student,
Having not known your green
From your brown.

Kortu:

Those are the utterances
Of an ungrateful student
Who got rusticated
From the grassland of the common
Universe to Graceland of the university.

Tigi:

A man like you should be made
To eat his words.

Kortu:

How do you feed a lion
If your hands tremble of weakness?

Tigi:

By throwing a punch at the face
Of a bad student like you.

Kortu:

> You dare not.
> Why do you hate so much for that
> Which does not touch you directly?
> This is Njai's fight not yours.
> It's suicidal.

Tigi:

> You come to my campus
> To steal a woman
> Far above your eyes.
> Fudia was the last woman
> You ever placed your hands on.

Kortu:

> Poor Tigi, leave if you wish to live!

Tigi:

> You come to the wrong campus
> With a big heart.
> When was it you signed
> The entry registrar of your
> Matriculation? *Mmmmmm,*
> I guess it is three weeks ago?
> The page
> In which the ink of the pen
> You signed your name with,
> Is yet to dry up on the paper, and now
> You are calling hell on yourself.
> Have it your way.

Kortu:

> You have grown so rustic
> On a campus

Meant to produce refined
People. After finishing with you,
I will spend the whole night finding
An explanation as to how
You survived four years of wretchedness.

Tigi commands his group to seize Kortu; but Kortu's group intercepts and a wrestle begins. The group except Tigi and Kortu fight each other for supremacy. Knives begin to flash from among them and soon blood begins to drip. The violence leaves one person from each group stabbed while the rest run away. Tigi takes out a gun and so does Kortu. They aim at each other and fire. Kortu, and Tigi scream…and both fall dead.

THE CURTAIN FALLS

ACT TWO
SCENE ONE

The scene opens in a diner. There are about twelve guests of men and women in at least four tables. A somber music plays in the background. Otherwise the atmosphere is calm and serene. Cigarette smoke disappears in the air. A few occasionally gyrate to the music before returning to their seats. Falilu, Fudia and Khadija walk into the diner, surveying the environment before settling for somewhere to sit.

Khadija:

> Fudia don't you remember
> We came to this place
> On a weekend four years ago
> When we just entered college?

Fudia:

> How time flies.
> Someone has a lasting memory
> Of this place...
> And who is that?

Falilu:

> That would be me *meeeee!*
> I met my wonderful Khadija
> Here four years
> Three bottles of beers ago.
> *They laugh.*

Prof. Sankoh:

> *He walks over to their table.*
> It is quite a place
> For a college closure.

Fudia:

    Professor Sankoh!!! So you are here?

Prof. Sankoh:

    I came in here a few hours ago…

    Just saw you guys from the counter.

    A waiter approaches with a tray of assorted drinks and serves the table. Fudia and Khadija order while Falilu and Professor Sankoh open beers.

    What is this trio celebrating tonight?

    Fudia and Khadija are adding

    To the glamour of tonight…

Khadija

    Our apparent exit from the university

    To the multiversity, how about that

    Professor Sankoh.

Professor Sankoh:

    Little wonder whether we need

    The electrical bulbs

    Where these human bulbs glow?

    They laugh.

Falilu:

    Prof, after four years of hard labor

    At the university toiling,

    Please tell me

    Who would not want

    To celebrate?

Prof. Sankoh:

    It was toil well worth it.

    He reaches for his drink.

    To what are we drinking tonight?

Falilu:

To everything collegial, to you
Professor Sankoh
Who nurtured us to hold
Our voices in academia through
Practical criticism, to us the rest
Of mankind for daring this far.

Fudia:

I want to drink to enlightenment.
I want to gulp a big bottle
Of a good wine to that effect.

Falilu:

That big bottle of wine is on me,
And I know which exactly
Will make your day, Fudia.

Fudia:

Aahahahahaha that should be so nice.

Khadija:

Fudia, if it's *Pure Heaven*,
You can be sure I will join you.

Falilu:

That's my girl.
And *Pure Heaven* it will be.
Waitress, please two
Of chilly *Pure Heaven!*
*In that instance a popular song that gets everyone ready to
dance hits the box. Khadija asks Professor Sankoh to a
dance while Falilu asks Fudia to a dance. They join the
number of other dancers on the floor. After the music stops
they take their seats. Falilu asks to be excused and goes to*

> *the gents. After a while he returns to the table and finds the group chatting. He waits for the music to subside and moves to the center of the hall.*

Falilu:

Ladies and gentlemen,
I know this is not your usual party
To which we were all invited by anyone;
Therefore, I crave your indulgence
To grant me a brief moment to take your time…
The diner remains quiet. Looking around him.
Very well, very well. I appreciate,
I appreciate.
There is a quick shout of support. The place goes quiet.

Fudia:

Go for it!

Falilu:

Seriously, I appreciate, I appreciate.
Tonight some of us here,
Students at the university are celebrating
The end of our final examinations…
Meaning, if we make it,
We will be decorated
With university qualifications.
So, in the first place,
I want to shout out to all potential
Graduates in the coming weeks.
A wild applause of support goes up.
Today, ladies and gentlemen,
As I celebrate the end of one chapter
In my life, I implore you to join me

And to support my courage,
As, without notice to anyone,
Pauses, he moves toward his table.
I ask a lady over there
To consider me when
I decide to ask her parents
For her hand in marriage.

He moves over to Khadija, stands over her. Khadija is clearly surprised. Her hands are on her mouth as if to block any sound of excitement. She takes a quick look at Fudia who nods her head in excitement. Falilu kneels.

Before God and man,
I wish to say that after dating you
For four years on college campus,
I am pleased to inform you that
I will be honored if you were to marry me.

Khadija takes the hand of Falilu, embraces him, and both dance to the soft music. Applauses go up in the air. At the end of the music, Khadija takes hold of Falilu's hand and they both flee the stage excitedly. In that moment, Njai dramatically enters the diner, clapping his hands. All attention turns to him. The diner remains silent.

Njai:

Today is the day when men shall
Be men, and women would be won
By those who deserve them.
My heart burns for someone,
For a lady of the moon.
She steps on my alacrity and
I brought her unto my wavelength.

The gods speed me up.
He turns to the table of Fudia.
Fudia, my love, today is the day which the Lord
Has made...I will rejoice and be glad in it.
May I please beseech you to join me
On the dance floor?
*Silence ensues, and in that moment, Fudia rises. The others
applaud. Fudia walks majestically to join Njai. After a
brief whispering, Njai turns to his audience.*
Ladies and Gentlemen,
When I entered that door,
I only represented myself
And now as I speak to you,
I represent myself and Madam Fudia...
*Falilu and Khadija return to the scene not knowing what is
going on.*

Falilu:

What have we missed?

Njai:

Oh, you two are here.
Congratulations on your examination,
And for what else
Must I congratulate you?

Falilu:

S*tern.*
And what's the occasion?

Njai:

To perform to her
The honor I just missed
You performing to Khadijah...

Falilu:
> Do you mean to….

Fudia:
> Stop Falilu!
> I need to give him a chance.
> I need to listen to him…
> To punish him with my patience…
> To make him want to come back
> Even as he keeps falling.
> *She closes up with Njai and looks into his eyes keenly.*
> A man who falls often is reminded
> By each fall that he can rise again.

Falilu:
> Very well, dear Fudia.
> *He turns to Njai*
> Now, you have the fall, Njai, fall again.
> It is not my wish for you to fall,
> Even again and again.
> *He closes in on Njai*
> Buddy, could you for this moment
> And every other moment
> Learn to rise and rise?
> For her happiness, I wish for you
> To rise and rise and rise.
> *He turns to the others.*
> For the happiness of a serene
> And chaste Fudia,
> I wish for Njai to rise and rise and rise!
> Now join me you good people,
> For her happiness, I wish for you

to rise and rise and rise!

The chorus thunders "rise and rise and rise!" three times. Njai turns to Fudia, kneels and takes a pouch from his breasts pocket. He looks up to Fudia.

Njai:

He shouts with emotions.

Fudia, will you marry me?

Fudia screams long and loud, takes Njai up and embraces him. In that moment a group of campus security shows up, walk up to Njai.

Security:

Sir, we hate to disrupt

Such a nice gathering...

But we are here because

You have decided

To break from your suspension

From campus in connection with

The deaths of Tigi,

Kortu and others

Now being investigated.

Prof. Sankoh:

Hey, what is going on here?

These are students of the university.

I hope there is no problem?

Security:

I'm afraid sir, there's a problem.

We have our orders

To keep Mr. Njai

From coming to this campus.

We understand he's on suspension

Related to murder cases from which
He's broken his suspension.

Njai:

I have never been charged
With anything related to that because
I am not responsible for that.

Security:

Sir it is not for us to say,
But if you will respectfully follow us
Off the campus, I think you might
Have an opportunity to continue
Discussion with madam later.

Prof. Sankoh:

Come with me Njai.
I will follow up on your matter
With the university authorities.

Fudia:

Njai, go in peace with them,
I am confident you will be exonerated
And yes, I will marry you,
Yes, I will marry you today
And I will marry you forever!

She sobs. Security arrests Njai and walk off scene with him. The guests continue to clap for the proposal until the scene closes.

THE CURTAIN FALLS

ACT TWO
SCENE TWO

The scene opens at a private residence, a neatly arranged parlor. In a corner of the palor, a man, aged 65 years offers a silent Muslim prayer. The adult, Alhaji Majid finishes his prayers and returns to his big chair. After a while, Isatu, a hesitant teenage girl in hijab, enters and respectfully kneels before Alhjai Majid.

Alhaji Majid:

Speak, I hear you!

Isatu:

Uncle, a lady waits outside
to speak to you, sir.

Alhaji Majid:

Where is she coming from
And how is she dressed?

Isatu:

She didn't say sir.
She pauses.
She does not have the hijab on, sir.

Alhaji Majid:

She comes to me bear headed?
What is it she wants?

Isatu:

She did not tell me.
She pauses.

Alhaji Majid:

Girls will never learn the important
Things that turn them into women.

How can you forget the important lesson
In life that I teach you?
C'mon go and ask her to speak
To your mother.
You inferior thing!
Isatu rises to go.
Wait! Since I do not know what
She wants, ask your mother to meet
With her here.
I will be in my room.
Isatu dashes out while Alhaji Majid leaves the scene for his room. In a moment, the mother enters and is followed by Fudia.

Mother:

Take a sit, my daughter.
Have you eaten anything yet?

Fudia:

Yes, Ma'am,
I ate before coming here.

Mother:

I hope you did not
Go through any problem
To find the house?

Fudia:

No, Ma'am, I did not.
After a pause.
Ma'am, I am here because of Khadija.

Mother:

You said
You are here on behalf

Of my daughter, Khadija?
Did she send you?

Fudia:

Em, em em, she has not sent me, Ma'am.

Mother:

So you are here on behalf of her interest.
How do you mean?

Fudia:

No, no, ma'am, I can't do this...
Maybe I should go back.

Mother:

She lays her palm on her chest.
My heart, my heart, oh my heart...
Is anything wrong with her?

Fudia:

No, no, nothing is wrong with her...
Although something is wrong, and unless
You stop it from happening,
It could be wrong with her for a long time.

Mother:

She rises from her chair, shouting.
Somebody come and hold my head!
O! What is it this young lady is bringing
Upon my head? *ooooo.*

Alhaji Majid:

Alhaji Majid is drawn to the living room.
What is the matter?

Mother:

Whoever this lady is I don't know.
She just walked up to me

To tell me
That my daughter, Khadija is in trouble!
ohhhhhh my people.
Please ask her for me what kind of trouble
Is she in *ohhhhhh?*
Is she involved
In an accident?
Alhaji, Alhaji, where are you?
Speak please, say something!

Alhaji Majid:

Wait a minute Mother of Khadija,
Wait a minute.
Sits in his chair and turns to Fudia.
What is the problem with my daughter?

Fudia:

Hysterical
It is nothing, sir.

Alhaji Majid:

What do you mean, nothing,
And her mother is shouting restlessly?

Fudia:

I just didn't know how to put it,
But I didn't mean to upset her.

Alhaji Majid:

Well, I'm waiting,
Try to find a better way
Of putting it before
My wife drops dead here
In front of your eyes.
I'm waiting...

Fudia:

> Okay, okay, okay sir!
> *She screams.*
> You all stop causing noise!
> *Instant quietness*
> Listen, I didn't
> Come here to kill anyone
> Or to upset anyone.
> I am here because
> Khadija is my friend
> And I mean well for her.
> *She pauses and looks around her*
> Khadija is a blessed child
> Because of this home
> She comes from.
> I never knew you, her family,
> But you have shown me that
> You care for her welfare.

Mother:

> She is our only daughter,
> And we want her to grow
> Into a good child.

Fudia:

> I know you all also
> Want her to grow
> Into a responsible child, into a leader
> In this country. You want her
> To be highly educated.
> To be…to be…to be…the president
> Of this country.

Mother:

> We want her to be
> A good mother
> And wife to her husband.

Alhaji Majid:

> Can you please
> Tell us why you are here?

Fudia:

> That's it, mother of Khadija...
> You see, she doesn't want to be a good
> Wife or a good mother....

Alhaji Majid & Mother:

> What?
> *The parents scream in frustration.*

Fudia:

> No, no, no that's not what I mean.
> Yes, she should be a good wife and
> A good mother.
> I too want to be a good
> Wife and a good mother; but, but,
> But Khadija and I want to be the good
> Wife and the good mother
> That we choose to be.

Alhaji Majid:

> So is that what Khadija wants
> You to come and tell us?
> You woman without a hijab,
> I hope you are not a friend
> Of my daughter?
> Khadija has a future

Carved out in this home and
Who are you to come and change it?

Fudia:

You cannot marry off Khadija
To the man you want
To without her consent.
In fact, she does not know the man
And how can you expect
Her to marry him?

Alhaji Majid:

Lahilah-lala, Muhammadu Rasululaa…
Why is this ill luck
Happening to my family?

Fudia:

What ill luck sir?

Alhaji Majid:

Don't talk back to me!

Fudia:

God forbid!
I wouldn't dare talk back to you, sir.
You are my father's age.
Alhaji Majid paces.

Mother:

Where is my daughter, Khadija?
She shakily walks away from the scene.

Fudia:

She should be on campus.

Alhaji Majid:

Campus, doing what?
Don't you fear God?

Fudia:

> I fear God so much and
> I do not mean any harm to Khadija.

Alhaji Majid:

> How come you want to lead
> My daughter astray?

Mother:

> *She enters the scene.*
> I have tried to call Khadija
> But she did not pick up.
> Daughter of whoever, would
> You tell me why
> She is not picking up?
> Where did you take her?
> *She sobs.*
> My only daughter *ohhhhhh*,
> My only daughter.

Isatu:

> *Isatu dashes into the scene without her hijab.*
> Are you here to send my aunt
> To her grave, early?

Fudia:

> Far from that, lady.

Isatu:

> *Speaks aggressively and rudely claps her hands.*
> Looks very much like that.
> You must go through me to achieve
> Your goal.
> Why are you so concerned
> About who Khadija marries or not?

Does that decision sit
On your throbbing heart?
What daylight witch are you?

Fudia:

You do not understand that
I have an interest in Kadija's affairs.
I am here to look into her interest.
The man her parents want to marry
Your cousin to, has no emotional
Relationship with her.
Khadija is a big
And educated lady that, at her age,
Knows what she wants.
I am sure you can speak
That truth to your uncle.

Alhaji Majid:

Young lady, I think you must leave
Now, you have overstayed your visit.
Thank you for turning
My house upside down.

Isatu:

Leave, just leave.
You heard my uncle.
Fudia quickly walks out of the house.

THE CURTAIN FALLS

ACT TWO
SCENE THREE

Fudia paces her room looking like a disturbed woman. In a moment Falilu rudely enters, angry as a storm.

Falilu:

Fudia, did you go to
Khadija's family house?

Fudia

Sit down.
Let's talk about it.

Falilu:

Talk about what?
Is it true about all
Your misbehavior there?

Fudia:

You need to hear
The full story from me.
Just take a seat, please.

Falilu:

What is wrong with you?
How can you be so callous?
Why did you go
To Khadija's home to cause
Her problems? Are you mad?

Fudia:

I was just trying to be of help to her.

Falilu:

Oh yeah? How?
By destroying her future?

69

Fudia:

> Can't you see she has
> No future with her parents?

Falilu:

> And you find yourself in the best
> Possible position to determine
> What is good for her future, right?
> Have you gone mad?

Fudia:

> This is not right that you must
> Question my good intention.

Falilu:

> It's called *goof* intention.
> That's what it is called, *goof* intention.
> You goofed and turned everyone's world
> Upside down—and now you
> Are incapable of healing the wounds.

Fudia:

> Is it right that an educated girl like
> Khadija should have her
> World planned
> For her without her knowing it?

Falilu:

> What do you know?
> How do you mean to play a role
> For another person when you cannot
> Even play it for yourself?

Fudia:

> Yes, I knew it. I knew it, that you
> Have been harboring these sentiments

Against me. You wanted to tell me
And now you have the chance to do it.

Falilu:

I don't care how you wish to interpret
It but if I were you
I would fix my own life
And leave others to fix theirs.

Fudia:

Don't you come to my room to try
To insult me. I am a grown up and
Can take care of myself.
Give me a break, Mr. Righteous!

Falilu:

You have just destroyed the life
Of a young lady in one single day.

Fudia:

I did no such thing.
If anything
I have helped her to confront
Her own fears,
And that should give her the courage
To speak the truth to her parents.

Falilu:

What truth? I wish you were
Smart enough to put
Yourself in her shoes.

Fudia:

Don't tell me that.
What do you know about the shoes
I wear, or for that matter,

Shoes people like Khadija and other
Women wear?
You think I wish to be with
Every man I meet on the street
Or on this campus? You think
I'm so insecure that I always want
To have a man beside me? What do
You know about a woman's shoes?
Give me a break.
She falls on her knees and sobs bitterly.
I did it all in good faith for you,
My childhood friend.
How we grew up together
Meaning well for each other,
Never hurting each other.
Is this the price
I pay for trying to save your relationship?
What shall I do now?
What shall I do now?

Falilu:

Softens.
Why didn't you tell me about
Your plans to go to Khadija's house?

Fudia:

She told me she didn't want
You to know.
She thought she was going
To be able
To manage her parents and
Handle the matter her way.

Falilu:

> That is until you came and
> Messed up everything.

Fudia:

> You don't understand,
> I didn't want
> Her to repeat her class just because
> She feared her parents were intending
> To marry her off after college.

Falilu:

> What are you talking about?
> Where's that coming from?

Fudia:

> This was what she didn't
> Want you to know.
> She was confused about it and
> Was finding a way to rebel.
> The first thought that came
> Into her head was to repeat her class,
> Which would have
> Delayed or frustrated
> Her parents from marrying
> Her off this year.

Falilu:

> *Almost to himself*
> I don't believe this.
> Oh my God!

Fudia:

> So you see, I had no choice
> But to try to save the situation.

Falilu:

Sternly.
Yes, you had a choice.
You had
The choice of sharing that
Information with me before you
Went and did something stupid.

Fudia:

She stopped me from doing that.
I needed her to trust me if I was going
To help the two of you find a way
To address the situation.

Falilu:

And you don't care that
I should trust you?

Fudia:

I have never ever dreamt of any
Distrust between the two of us
Because the circumstances have never
Warranted it. But I needed
To give her my word.

Falilu:

Well, you can be sure now that I have
Lost any trust I had in you.

Fudia:

Has it come to that now?

Falilu:

Trust.
Yes, trust is the watch word here.
Did I go poking my nose

Into anyone about you and Kortu,
That first year student?
Fudia remains silent.
Anything I might have said could
Have made the matter
Worse than it ended.
I always believe that if I had to talk
To you alone, I should do
That to protect your interest.
Now, see how you have blown
Up the matter between Khadija and me.
He paces
I am worried what angles the matter
Would take now that Khadija's parents
Are suspicious that she had been
Opposed to their plans.

Fudia:

I may have done what you and
Khadija didn't expect but it might just
Turn out to be
The catalyst to getting
The parents
To come to terms with reality.

Falilu:

I'm always fascinated by your
Reckless optimism that things always
Find ways of righting their wrongs.
He removes his phone from his pocket
Let me try to reach Khadija to see
If there is more

To the matter right now.
The phone rings for a moment and goes to voice mail.
She's not picking her phone.
God knows what anger she could
Be buried in right now.

Fudia:

Maybe I should visit her room
Later tonight and talk
To her about the matter.

Falilu:

No. No, I don't believe that's
The right thing for you to do.
If anything, please stay out
Of her sight until
I have first seen and talked to her.

Fudia:

Can I ask you a question?

Falilu:

As long as it is not about you taking
The first action.

Fudia:

Did Khadija
Ever give you a reason
To fear her family?

Falilu:

What kind of a question is that?

Fudia:

Listen, I know it's going to get
Worse before it gets better;
But I discovered today that

Khadija's parents are vulnerable
With respect to Khadija.

Falilu:

How do you mean?

Fudia:

They are not going to hurt her.
In fact, I believe that they are now
In fear that their little conspiracy
Might land them
Into trouble if Khadija
Should turn out to be angry
With them for manipulating her.

Falilu:

In shock
I don't believe this!
Are you the Fudia
I grew up with? You have become
So strange in thoughts and in action.
I have to leave now before
I get angry again.
He leaves. Fudia paces a few moments before the scene fades.

THE CURTAINS FALL

ACT TWO
SCENE FOUR

Fudia circles the field two times, sometimes nodding and other times shaking her head.

Fudia:

Have I become a victim
Of my own education?
Has the vault of higher learning blinded
Me in the eyes? Even my childhood
Friend thinks I am different
From the Fudia who came
To the University four years ago.
What lightning struck me with an insatiate
Reaction to the body and the mind?
Am I guilty as charged? Guilty of a liberal mind
Or of a liberal self pity?

She gradually exits the scene; two children enter: a boy (Falilu age 13) and a girl (Fudia aged 11). The girl chases after the boy, until they both fall on the ground faking a wrestle. They then run in different directions.

Child Fudia:

Come on over here, Fudia!
Come and see what I found.

Child Falilu:

What is it, Falilu *liar ban*?

Child Fudia:

I found something you want?

He runs over to her, but before he reaches her she runs off to another spot. They do that two more times, then they skid.

Their feet become stuck under heavy rocks. Instantly he begins to cry. She painfully struggles to free her legs after which she turns to the crying Child Faliu and helps him free his foot too. He keeps crying.

Your leg is free now. Stop crying.

Child Falilu:

It's hurting me.

Child Fudia:

You just have to act like a big boy
And stop crying.

Child Falilu:

But I am not a big boy; it hurts.

Fudia runs to the thick of the forest, plucks a few leaves, grinds them and pours the contents where his leg pains. After a while he stops complaining.

Child Fudia:

Have you heard from
Good Boys' High School?

Child Falilu:

My mother
Went there yesterday
To check on the intake.
He throws a stone at a distance
She is told she still has to wait
And hope that those
Who met the school's
Grade are all accepted
Before they can
Consider my result.
He pauses

And you?

Have you heard from your school?

Child Fudia:

My letter of acceptance came

This morning from Good Girls' High School.

Child Falilu:

And you didn't tell me anything about that?

Child Fudia:

It's only this morning before you came

Dragging me to go for lessons.

Child Falilu:

Are you happy now?

Child Fudia:

Yes, of course I am happy now.

I am going to high school.

I am a big girl now.

She rises and walks like a grown up. He rises and walks to the end of the field in frustration. She goes to him.

Oh Falilu, I know you are worried

About your intake.

What can I do to help?

Child Falilu:

What *can* you do?

We are only kids.

Child Fudia:

But at least if I knew what to do I would try.

Child Falilu:

Well, that's it, part of being a grown up

Is to know what to do when with

Issues like this.

I'm sure my mum will do
Her best to get me into
Good Boys High School.
Child Fudia:
Can't you go to another school?
Child Falilu:
I can but you know I won't.
My older brothers went
To Good Boys' High;
So *I* have to go to Good Boys' High.
Child Fudia:
You will go to Good Boys' High.
Shall I tell my mum to help?
Child Falilu:
I'm sure my mum will ask your mum.
That's for grownups to decide.
They hold hands together as they exit the scene. After a
moment, Fudia enters the scene and stands in the center.
Fudia:
Why is my story changing?
Why?
Why is the story of Falilu
And me changing?
Here I am standing with more
Memories of our past,
Stories before we entered
University.
I know that university
Is meant to change us,
But that change is supposed

To be for the good.
Yes, I discovered long
Ago that the whole
Wild world could just
Have been fattening
In a vulnerable state, vulnerable
To mice of mortals threatening
Its atmospheric freedom,
Vulnerable to its
Own power of being.
Even in my simple world, my friends
And lovers eventually
Become vulnerable
To me, to my unencumbered self.
But there was a time
I was young and conforming
To everything
I heard from others.
She calls out aloud as she exits the scene.
Falilu! Falilu! Faliluuuuuu!
Do you now forsake me?
Enter two teenagers: Falilu, aged 17 and Fudia, aged 15.
They both have sandwiches they chew on occasionally.
Teen Falilu:
　Are you ready for university?
Teen Fudia:
　I am more than
　Ready for university.
　After a while
　Falilu, do you know

That our university
Has some ten thousand students?
Teen Falilu:
Wow! That's quite a number.
We have never been around such people
In one place. That must be a whole town.
Teen Fudia:
I guess that's why they call it a university.
It's like bringing together so many people
To think as if they are the universe.
Teen Falilu:
That's funny, but smartly put.
Teen Fudia:
I'm worried that I'll lose you
To that large number of students.
Teen Falilu
How can you talk like that
When our mission at the university
Is to make both
Mammy Fudia and Mammy Falilu
Proud? We want to be able
To make them comfortable
In their old age.
Teen Fudia:
Do you promise me?
Are we never going to go apart
From each other?
Teen Falilu:
Fudia!!! We have been through
This over and over.

You and I know we feel the same way.
We are going to go
To the university together and leave
There together in our academic gowns.

Teen Fudia:

I will walk so majestically beside
You with my degree in my hand that reads,
Bachelor of Arts in English with Honors!

Teen Falilu:

He is in shock
I don't understand.
You first opted to read sociology
How come
You are going to be in English with me?

Teen Fudia:

Why would
I want to offer something
Differently from what you offer?

Teen Falilu:

Oh my God, I don't believe it.
That's *so* you.

Teen Fudia:

We can't just go apart right now.
We started this battle together.

Teen Falilu:

Jokingly
Well,
I'm going to jump over to law.

Teen Fudia:

Hey Law, here I come.

Teen Falilu:

Mmmmmmm, well it's going

To be Education for *me*!

Teen Fudia:

Year, I guess we must

Choose to be teachers

To pay back to our community schools.

Teen Falilu:

Well, I have just changed my mind;

I will suspend my entry into the university.

Teen Fudia:

Mammy Falilu come *oooo*,

Your son is not going to

Enter university again.

Teen Falilu:

Mammy Fudia come *oooo*,

Your daughter does not know what

She wants to do at the university.

Teen Fudia:

You are nothing but trouble.

Teen Fudia chases Teen Falilu off stage.

CURTAIN FALLS

ACT THREE
SCENE ONE

At a local palm wine bar, sit two men with jugs of wine before them. The saleswoman paces about to arrange more guest seats.

Saleswoman:

Fɔni bɔbɔ.

Lɛk se i n ɔno wetin dis ples bi.

I de kam ya

Di kam aks fɔ tindɛm fɔlan.

Dis na skul?

Kongoma:

I luk lɛk dɛn

Bɔy dɛm na d univasiti.

Aw, I nɔ no se

dis na mampama bafa

ɛn nɔ to supamakit?

Kongosa:

Di buk we de

na in hed fiba lɛk univas.

We yu de tɔk

B tɔdi univasiti so,

Yu dɔn yɛri

di drama we de ɔp de.

Kongoma:

I!

Na ɔnli wan drama yu

no na d univasiti?

Kongosa:

>Wɛl, mi de tɔk bɔt di wan we ɔt,
>
>We ebribɔd de tɔk bɔt.

Kongoma:

>Tɛl mi ba wetin dis tɔng
>
>Nɔ de tɔk bɔt.
>
>Dɛn de tɔk bɔt wi we de alayv
>
>ɛn sɛf dɛn wan dɛm we dɔn day
>
>bɔt de fɔ sɛl.
>
>Pipul dɛn de day ɛbride
>
>Pipul dɛn de day tu msɔ
>
>ɛn na so sɛl de sɛl.

Kongosa:

>Wɛl wetin di univasiti witɔl di buk
>
>de du fɔ mek layf
>
>we wi fɔ de bay ɛn drink?
>
>Luk Kongosa in fes ba,
>
>awi sɔri fɔ luk.
>
>Di man nid niu wata layf naw fɔ drink.
>
>Kwik wan na in fes.
>
>Luk in nos,
>
>Luk aw di tin de blo,
>
>Fuku Faka, fuku faka
>
>Lɛk gru-mumu.

Saleswoman:

>Heiiii!
>
>Una blo!
>
>Una de tɔk tu mɔch, *masi*!
>
>*She pauses.*

A yɛri se di Pa we kin pas ya,
da Alhaji Pa in gial pikin,
Kadija, we de na univasiti
Dɔn *uummm?*
Ɛn in ɛn in papa di agiu oba
udat fɔ mared am?

Kongoma:

O! da wan de?
A! dat bin dɔn kɔmɔt
na do fɔ lɔng naw o

Saleswoman:

Yu fɔ dɔn no naw se wɛn
wɔd de pas pas arawnd fɔ
tu lɔng dat min se
Di tin stil de ɔn
Afta, afta afta dɛn tɔk am.
A yɛri se mɔ de
insay usay dat kɔmɔt.
Bɔt yu gɛt ɛn
niu tin insay di tori?

Kongosa:

Hei uman,
Wɛn wi kam na ya
Na mɔni we
Di pe fɔ drink ya
Nɔ to fri drink yu de gi wi.
If yu want mi padi
Fɔ Kɛrr-go-bring-kam
Na fɔ put di mampama

Saleswoman:

    Na yu biznɛs.

    Gbaraces!

    Wetin na mi yon de

    Pa hɔg mɔni

    We mi papa nɔ to bucha?

Kongoma:

    Madam, na mi yu fɔ yɛri to, *ya*.

    Infɔmeshɔn na fri skɔlaship naw.

    ɛm, ɛm, ɛm, yu d aks bɔt

    da bɔbɔ, we dɛn klɔ

    Kortu, ɛn di adɔwan,

    Tigi, we kil dɛn sɛf

    Na di univasiti rod?

Saleswoman:

    Dɛn bɔbɔ ya tide,

    go kil kil dɛn sɛf fɔ uman

    Bifo dɛn tray f ɔlan buk.

    Wetin do fɔ sɛn

    Pikin go kɔlɛg sɛf?

    Lɔng bifo dɛn lan buk.

    Way afɔ sɛn mipikin

    Na kɔlɛg?

Kongoma:

    Yu no se ɔda

    Studɛnt sɛf an

    Di na d kes de?

Kongosa:

    E*h* ɛ*h*, yɛs, a no.

Kongoma:

Da bɔbɔ

we dɛn kɔl Njai?

Da bɔbɔ de in hed nɔ de o!

Na mi Gɔd-dadi in pikin so.

Kongosa:

Gɔd-dadi?

Da man de na yu Gɔd?

Na yu Gɔd ɛn papa?

Kongoma:

No, no, no! Na mi Gɔdpapa

Nɔ to mi Gɔd ɛn papa.

Kongosa:

Btɔ yu jis tɔk am bak.

Na yu papagɔd ɛ*nti?*

Kongoma:

Ful man nɔ at fɔ no

A go jis mek lɛk yu nɔ de naya.

Madam, mek a kɔntiniu mi tori ya...

Kongosa:

Wɛl naw na tori yu de tɛl wi,

Nɔ to wetin yu no, ɛh?

Dis man dɔn drɔnk sɛf.

He laughs hysterically.

Saleswoman:

Bo tɔlk to mi bɛtɛ tin.

Nɔ lisin dis Kongoma man ya.

Kongosa:

Mi padi,

Yu tori dɔn bɔku naw o.

Way yu nɔ dɔn di fɔs tori

bifo wi kam to di ɔda tori

nadi kɔbɔd ɔf yu bren

ɛn tɛl wi di fɔs wan.

Wan tori at e taym,

So sez di Inglishman ɔ di British man.

Kongoma:

ɛ,ɛ, ɛ!

A go stat wit dis wan

ɛn cam ɔp to di fsɔ wan.

ɔ mek a stat wit di fnaw sɔ

ɛn cam dɔng to dis wan?

Tori bɔt Njai,

Mi Gdɔ-dadi in bnɔs yɔ

Kongosa:

ɛ!

*D*at Kongoma we de drink mampapma

Na Gɔd in pikin?

Kongoma:

He ignores Kongosa

Njai de jel na Padɛmba Rod.

Saleswoman:

Gboaayyyyy! *Argboreh!*

Bɔt i nɔ kil pɔsin o?

Kongoma:

Na di lɔ gɛt fɔ fɛn ntɔ bɔt dat.

Sɔntɛm I kil, Sɔntɛm I nɔ kil

To kil ɔ nɔt to kil,

91

So sez di Inglishman
ɔ di British man.
Kongosa:
Wetin na di difrɛns,
Inglishman ɛn British man?
Kongoma:
I like your question,
So sez di Inglishman
ɔ di British man.
Naw yɛri fayn fayn wan.
British na pɔsin
We dɛn bɔn na Briten.
Inglish man, na pɔsin we sabi Inglish.
Kongosa:
So, egen, wetin nadi difrɛns?
Kongoma:
I like your emphasis,
So sez di Inglishman ɔdi British man.
Naw yɛri egen.
Di Inglish man kin sabi spik Inglish
Bɔt I nɔ bɔn na Ingland.
Lɛk Mandɛla,
Lɛk Devidsin Nikul,
Lɛk Profɛsɔr ɛldrɛd Jons,
Lɛk Wole Soyinka
ɛn Chinua Achɛbɛ
ɔ ivin lɛk mi…
Bɔt di Inglish man
Bɔn na Ingland ɛn i sabi Inglish!

> *ɛh, ɛh, ɛh!*
>
> Eni ɔbjɛkshon?
>
> So sez di Inglishman ɔdi British man.
>
> *Eh, eh, eh!*
>
> *Any objection?*
>
> So sez di Inglishman ɔdi British man.

Kongosa:

> Tɛnki, tɛnki Kongoma.
>
> Naw mek wi go bak to yu tori.

Kongoma:

> *No, no, no!*
>
> *Not soon.*
>
> *Me deserve mampama service*
>
> *Me educated the house,*
>
> *So says the Englishman or the British man.*

Kongosa:

> *Okay, Madam, service we again.*

Kongoma:

> *Madam serves a round.*
>
> Dɛn fɛn wan lɛta we prov se
>
> Njai na in ɔda di kilin.
>
> Fɔ kil fɔ in gialfrɛn.
>
> Pyɔnt ɔf kɔrɛkshɔn ɔr
>
> kɔrɔpshɔn.
>
> Di lɛta alɛgɛdli prov se
>
> Na Njai ɔda di kilin,
>
> So sez di Inglishman ɔdi British man.

Kongosa:

> *Annoyingly*
>
> Yu want fɔ se lɛk we a d drink

Mampama naw ɛn yu de si mi,
Koro koro wan,
Yu wan fɔ tɛl mi se
Na alɛgɛdli ade alɛgɛdli, drink?

Kongoma:

Now I know I am an educated man,
And Kongosa is not.

Saleswoman:

Ignoring Kongosa

A yɛri se dɛn mit am
Di konani mared to di uman
We ikil fɔ,
Na in dɛn arɛst am, *gbam*!

Kongosa:

Dɛn kech am rɔr ɔwan
na di univasiti ɛn dɛn lɔk
am ɔp fɔ tu wik wit flɔs lebɔ.

Kongoma:

He laughs and laughs and laughs.

Di Inglishman
ɔ di British man
Nɔ se fɔls lebɔ,
Di kɔrɛkt wan na *forced labor*.

Kongosa:

Na yu sabi, na yu lan buk.
Mi n ɔkia.
Na fɔs ɔ las lebɔ o, a n ɔkia...
Mek wi go bifo wit yu sabi.

Kongoma:

Di papa waka waka di kes

To plɛnti plɛnti pipul fɔ mek dɛn
Fri in pikin.

Kongosa:

Dat na yu Gɔd-dadi.

Amin yu se na Gɔd?

Way i fɔ waka waka fɔkes, ɛh?

Kongoma:

God don't like ugly o,
So sez di Inglishman
ɔdi British man.

Kongosa:

I lɛk biutiful ɛnti?

Kongoma:

Kwik kwik di kes go magistret kot
Frɔm de to ay kot.

Kongosa:

And then to lo Court?

Saleswoman:

eii wi di *kombra* dɛm!

I at o!

Di bɔbɔ
Dɔn mek fulishnɛs
Te i lɔs inbuk
We ide lan fɔ natin.

Kongoma:

Nɔ to fɔ natin o.
Na fɔ alɛgɛdli
spɔnsɔrin di kilin
ɔf in kɔ*mpin* dɛm.

Saleswoman:

>Kongoma, wetin apin wit
>
>Alaji Majid
>
>In gial pikin, Kadija?

Kongosa:

>No, no, no!
>
>No adɔtori ɔntil
>
>Wi gɛt fri savis
>
>Di f sɔtori
>
>Na bin fɔ fri, bɔt dis tori
>
>Wi nid fri bonɔs
>
>Savis ɔf mampama.

Saleswoman:

>Wɛl, du ya tekuna
>
>Fɛ sɔn las tori dɛm
>
>Kɔmɔt nia mi ba.
>
>A bin dɔn tɛl yu se
>
>Mi nɔkia bɔt univasiti
>
>Plaba we a nɔ wan de go de.

Kongoma:

>*He receives a cup full of palm wine from Saleswoman*
>
>Bo a dɔn tɛl yu,
>
>Nɔ lisin to Kongosa.
>
>Yu no wetin Kongosa min?
>
>*(Sings a song)*
>
>*Kongosa us tɛm yu go mared O*
>
>*Kongosa us tɛm yu go mared O*
>
>*Kongosa us tɛm yu go mared O*
>
>*Kongosa us tɛm yu go maredO*

Kongoma

> *Na pijin do me so*
> *Kongoma yɛtɛ ayɛtɛ Kongoma*
> *Tif mi nɔ tiff o*
> *Kongoma yɛtɛ ayɛtɛ Kongoma*
> *(Kongoma takes a big sip of his cup and belches.)*
> Madam, yu no se
> Di kes we Njai gɛt oda pipul dɛn
> Rop rop insai de?

Saleswoman:

> *Apɔko.*
> Na tru?

Kongosa:

> Na tru o mi sista.

Kongoma:

> Yu no se na wan big man
> Di pe kɔlɛg fi f ɔKadija?
> ɛn Alhaji bin dɔn prɔmis di man
> se afta kɔlɛg i go gi Kadija
> Di man fɔ mared?

Saleswoman:

> *Awo!*

Kongoma:

> Na so ooo!
> Dɛn wetin apin
> ɛn wetin n ɔapin,
> Wan adɔ gial pikin, a tink
> na in padi
> Go to di Alhaji in os
> ɛn go rɔn mɔt bɔt Kadija...

97

Kongosa:
>Dɔn di pa sɛf vɛx ya!

Kongoma:
>Na pikin vɛx?
>
>Kadija in mama
>
>Bi wan day wit at atak.

Saleswoman:
>Iiiii, watin apin so?

Kongosa:
>Mi n ɔno ooooooo.
>
>Yu nɔ yɛri di letɛst?

Saleswoman:
>Wetin na di letɛst naw?

Kongosa:
>Mi n ɔno oooo.

Kongoma:
>Wɛl, di po gial,
>
>Kadija nɔ go ebul
>
>Finish
>
>In univasiti egen ooooo.
>
>Alhaji Majid dɔn tek am
>
>Sɛn am go Gini
>
>Fɔ go mared di mared naw.

Saleswoman:
>Mmmmmmmmmm,
>
>Wnɔda nɔ go ɛva ɛnd.

Kongoma:
>Wɛl, tori go,
>
>Tori kam, tori
>
>lɛf pa Kongosa.

Mek mi de go na os ya

Fɔ go it mi *sakiɲmbɔy.*

Saleswoman:

Yu nɔ pe mi et o Kongosa.

pe mi ba, pe mi.

Kongoma:

Tide na mi de pe.

Tumara na Kongosa.

Ya, gi mi cheng.

THE CURTAIN FALLS

ACT THREE
SCENE TWO

The scene opens to an empty intersection. Kongosa and Kongoma enter. There was an instant thunderous sound of applause that scare the two men, sending them crashing about in fear. A voice comes on a microphone.

Voice:

"Therefore, I want to challenge and
Admonish you all to live up
To the expectations of the university.
While many of you will go out into the real
Universe and find ways of applying
The knowledge gained at the university,
Others will stay here and move
On to higher heights. Whatever you do,
Remember that you are going
To be forever measured by the depth
Of your education and the University
Of your education."

There is another round of applause. At this point, Kongosa and Kongoma begin, unsuccessfully, to trace where the speech and applause are coming from. But it seems to be coming from everywhere. The speech resumes.

"Alexander Pope, the eighteenth century
English poet, in the context of using
The mythical river, the Pierian Spring
As a metaphor, a river said to have been
Based in Macedonia, where the more
One drank of the water, the more

Knowledgeable one became, noted
In his "Essay on Criticism"
As follows: 'A little learning
Is a dangerous thing/Drink deep or taste
Not the Pieriain Spring/There shallow
Draughts intoxicate the brain/And
Drinking largely sobers us again.'
As I conclude, on behalf
Of the university and myself, I wish you all,
Individually as well as collectively,
A successful journey to the class of 2017."
*Another thunderous round of applause and bellows of
support for the speaker soars from among the graduating
class and holding for a while; they sing the university song.*

Kongosa:

Wetin di apin?
I fiba lɛk pipul dɛn de go wa.

Kongoma:

He laughs out
Mmmmm, wa naw…
Na buk wa.
Nobɔdi nɔ de day o.

Kongosa:

Na dat gɛt ɔl da kayn na ba ned zyɔ?

Kongoma:

Yɛs, ɔf kzɔ.
Pipul spɛnd lɔng tɛm na dis ples
Fɔ lan.
Wɛn dɛm finish wɛl, wɛl dɛm
go gladi gladi.

As the voices of students approach, Kongosa and Kongoma quickly exit the scene. Soon, some fifteen graduating class members, in their gowns, begin to pace the scene, chatting in groups. That goes on for a while until all the class disappears from the scene. At that moment Kongosa and Kongoma reappear in the scene.

Kongosa:

Dɛn ivin wɛrr ashɔbi

lɛk se na mared okeshɔn.

Kongoma:

Yɛs, na lɛk dɛn don mared

to buk gud gud wan.

Kongosa:

He sighs.

A! if mi papa bin put mi

Skul, lɛk a de wɛrr dis kayn ashɔbi

Fɔ sho se a dɔn lan buk gud gud wan.

He imitates

A fɔ bin de mas di grɔn

af af lɛk Inglishman ɔ British man.

Kongoma:

Nɔ drim yanda mi frɛn.

Yu hed sɛf sho se dɛm

Nɔ mek am fɔ buk.

Kongosa:

Yu nɔ si

wan gradwet in hed?

I fiba lɛk sup bol.

Mi yon bɛtɛ sɛf.

Instantly, Fudia, in her graduation gown, enters in haste unsure what direction to go. She attempts all directions but gets stuck in the middle of the stage. She notices Kongosa and Kongoma and sighs.

Fudia:

Oh, I don't know which way to go.

Kongoma:

What?
The road shortly to my left
Will go longly to my right.
Then, when if you follow it until
Far far from me you will leave it
Or take it to my nearness quick quick.
Then take it to your college where
You *kɔmɔt* with it.

Fudia:

Thank you sir.
To herself
I wish I knew
What he is talking about
It's just that I am confused;
I need to see
Someone soon, to talk
To him….to…to..to….

Kongosa:

To Kongoma
Way yu nɔ tɔk to di gial na krio?
Naw a shɔ se
Yu big big grama
Dɔn mek in hed dɔn at.

Kongoma:

> *Half proud, half embarrassed*
>
> Yɛs, yu rayt.
>
> Na ɔnli jsɔ a smɔl pikin.
>
> Mek a tɔk smɔl smɔl Krio grama.

Kongosa:

> Wɛl go tɔk to ram nɔ
>
> Mek I nɔ kray.

Kongoma:

> *Approaching Fudia*
>
> Oke, oke, oke a ɔndastand.
>
> Yu kɔmpin dɛm bin de
>
> Na ya bɔt dɛn
>
> ɔl dɔn go dat we.
>
> So go dat way?

Fudia:

> Sorry, that was not what I meant.
>
> But, oh, first,
>
> I don't like to be too rude;
>
> My name is Fudia, and
>
> What about you guys?

Kongoma:

> Mi nem Kongoma.

Kongosa:

> Mi na Kongosa.

Fudia:

> It is a pleasure
>
> To meet you both.
>
> I graduated today after
>
> Four years of study

At this university.
She pauses.
Do you guys work here?

Kongosa:

No, wi nɔ de wɔk ya.
Wi de na tawn.

Fudia:

Oh, I get it. You are the guys
Who came to see us graduate, right?
Who invited you?

Kongoma:

Nobɔdi nɔ invayt wi.

Kongosa:

Nɔ, dat nɔ to tru,
di ɛdmasta invayt wi.

Fudia:

Di headmaster?
Oh, that will
Be the Vice Chancellor.

Kongosa:

Yɛs, Mr. Chanci Yɔn,
di Chayniz bɔs.

Kongoma:

Taps Kongosa on his head.
Di University Vice Chancellor
N ot ɔChayniz man.

Fudia:

She giggles while her right hand covers her mouth.
I see, so you work
For the Chinese company

Constructing our university?
You guys
Build the roads around town?

Kongosa:

Yɛs, na wi di bil,

Di bil ɔl di ples.

She goes to join them and sits on a raised bench in one corner.

Fudia:

I wish on a day like this
That I have graduated,
I can say I am a happy lady.
But I'm not;
I'm not a happy lady.
My heart is bleeding.

Kongosa:

Yu de blid!

Wetin apin?

Yu wund?

Usay d blid de?

Fudia:

She stares at Kongosa.

Yes,
I am wounded at heart.
My love couldn't graduate.
I wish he was here with me.
She rises and walks to the center; turns around to face Kongosa and Kongoma.
I wish my true love,
Njai was here to see me in this attire.

I wish he too was receiving
His own degree.
I would have been so the happier.

Kongosa and Kongoma:

Both together.

Njai! Njai!!

Fudia:

In shock.

Yes, yes, Njai my love.
Do you guys know him?

Kongosa:

Wɛl, wɛl... wɛl, wɛl.

Kongoma:

Mi padi no am
Lɛk aw in mtɔ
no mampama.
Na Kongosa in Gɔd-dadi pikin.

Fudia:

I need him right now here
To share my degree
With him, to touch
Him till tomorrow come.

Kongosa:

Bɔt *eiii* Papa Gɔd, Njai dɔn go na jel
na Padɛmba Rod oo!

Fudia:

I know that my dear,
And he is in jail,
Even so unjustifiably.
She paces.

Njai didn't kill
Or planned
The killing of anyone.

Kongosa:

Na tru o, na tru.
Kongoma ivin tɔk am se
Na alɛgɛdi Njai kil di pipul dɛm.

Fudia:

She turns furious
What?
How can you say
Such a vicious thing
About someone you don't know?
Don't you know
It's a false accusation?
What is alleged
About the lies heaped
On the head of my boyfriend.

Kongosa:

A beg padin mi sista.
A nɔ min bad.
Na grama
We a lan frɔm Kongoma.
To Kongoma
If yu nɔ kiaful
Wit yu lay lay grama
Da Inglishman ɔ British man
We yu lɛk fɔ falamaka
Go mek wan de
Dɛn put mi na Bambakayaka

Fudia:

> That's okay.

Kongoma:

> A wish wi kin do sɔmtin fɔ ɛp
>
> Mek yu gɛt bak yu man.
>
> Wi nɔ min bad fɔ yu at ɔl.

Fudia:

> As a matter of fact,
>
> To appease my heart, there is something
>
> I think you could do.
>
> I need to communicate
>
> With Njai.
>
> I need to feel for him
>
> And him for me.

Kongosa:

> Wetin wi fɔ do fɔ yu, madam?.

Fudia:

> I want you to go to his jail
>
> And find out everything about him for me.
>
> I need my love to reach him through you.

Kongosa:

> *Chai!*
>
> Mek wi tek yu lɔv to Njai?
>
> Mek wi visit am?

Kongoma:

> Yɛs,
>
> Fudia wi go visit yu bɔyfrɛn.
>
> Sɛnd wi naw.

Kongosa:

> Wi go kɛrr yu lɔv to him fɔ yu.

Fudia:

> I was going to go there myself.
> I was going to visit him until I was told
> That Njai will not be allowed
> Any visitor because he is kept under
> Tight protection as they do to people
> Charged with murder.

Kongoma:

> Wi go si am bay Gɔd in pawa!

Fudia:

> *She removes an envelope from her side pocket.*
> I want him to have this letter.
> It has everything, everything:
> My love, my tears
> My blood, my sweat—my all.
> Here, take this small amount
> For your trouble.
> I can never thank you well.
> After you deliver,
> I want you guys to meet
> Me here tonight.
> I want to ask you
> To do another
> Assignment tonight
> At the same Pademba Prisons.
> Both of you come closer.
> Let me whisper in your ears.
> Walls have their own ears.
> *Kongosa and Kongoma move closer to Fudia. She whispers*
> *in their ears.*

Kongosa:

> Wi dɔn *yɛri* yu.
>
> *Fudia hugs Kongosa and Kongoma before they exit the scene. She paces back and forth and after a while exits:*

THE CURTAIN FALLS

ACT THREE
SCENE THREE

Falilu enters the scene, confused. He is still dressed in his graduation gown. He paces back and forth, pulling his hair. He removes his phone and tries to make calls but nobody picks on the other end.

Falilu:

He repeats a call on his phone.

Please Khadija pick up your phone!

Where are you?

I am dying for you.

Pick up the phone, please!

He drops the hand he holds the phone in frustration. Suddenly the phone rings.

Khadija!

Khadija! Is that you?

Speak up please!

He pauses.

Sorry, who? Oh, Isatu it is you?

Have you seen Khadija yet?

Pauses.

Oh no!

Okay, I am here, please meet me

Let us plan what next to do.

Okay, I'll be here.

He tries Khadija's number a few more times but no answer comes through. Isatu enters the scene.

Isatu:

Falilu, I hope you are doing okay?

Falilu:

How can I, Isatu, how can I?
Not until I find Khadija.

Isatu:

You shouldn't have allowed that lady
To go to our house and talk to
My uncle and aunt as she did.

Falilu:

How could I have done
Something like that?
Fudia is my childhood friend.
I don't know how she ended up
Visiting your house.

Isatu:

Anyway staying here wouldn't help
Us trace Khadija.
I have tried reaching
Some of her closest friends and nobody
Has seen her since yesterday.
Let me go get some more
Information from
Home and I will join
You to search for her.

Falilu:

Okay, I will wait here until you
Come back…but please make sure
Your phone is alive in case
I need to reach you.

Isatu:

Very well.

Falilu and Isatu exit the scene in different direction.
In that moment, enter Kongosa and Kongoma

Kongoma:

Yu shɔ se wi go sɔksid fɔ gɛt Njai awt
so dat Fudia go tɔk to ram?

Kongosa:

Bɔt yu yɛri wetin di ɔfisa se.
I se I nɔ go izi o. Na dat mek
I aks fɔ da kaynd amawnt ɔf mɔni de.

Kongoma:

So na fɔ da ledi dɛn studɛnt
Dɛm go kil dɛnsɛf?

Kongosa:

Kongoma, da we we da gial fayn,
a fit kil yu fɔ ram, misɛf.

Kongoma:

Na watin go na yu hed?
Na yu nɔ m ɔfɔ gɛt fayn gial?

Kongosa:

Me hed krak sɛf a go kil fɔ ram.

Kongoma:

Kongosa lɛf fɔ de drim ya.
Go fɔs na klas wan
Ba mek yu sabi rid
ABCD bifo yu kam timap bifo
Da univasiti uman tɛl am plɛnti tɔk.

Kongosa:

Dɛn se Bailɔ Bari yu se
Davidsin Nikul. Yu nɔ no se

If a gɛt mɔni, na tri univasiti

uman dɛm a de put na os?

Kongoma:

Nɔ fɔgɛt se yu gɛt

Dɛt to Seluman o fɔ in mampama.

Kongosa:

A!

Nɔ to tu mɔch.

Tide na mi tɔn

Fɔ bay di mampama.

A go pe am ɔl.

A phone rings.

Na yu fon de ring so.

Kongoma:

Hɛlo Mr. ɔfisa....

Yɛs na mi de tɔk....hɛlo.....

Sɔri na di nɛtwɔk.

Kongosa:

O *Salonesɛ*!

Dɛn layn ɔlwez bad.

Kongoma:

Wet, Kongoma....mek a yɛri fayn.

Yɛs, a de gɛt yu ....

ɔmɔs yu se wi fɔ pe yu?

No, wi jis wan fɔ mek

Yu pul am mek i kam si in gialfrɛn.

He pauses.

Nɔ, i nɔ go bi fɔ wan awa sɛf. ...

Yɛs, wi go lɛk dat fɔ apin

Na nɛt…. Oke ɔfisa wi de kam na nɛt.

The phone cuts off the call.

Yɛs! Wi dɔn sɔksid!

He gives Kongosa a high five.

Di ɔfisa wan fɔ mek

Wi pe am Le150, 000.

I se na in de na nayt shift.

I gɛt fɔ sheb di mɔni wit

di ɔda nayt shift ɔfisa dɛm.

Kongosa:

Le150, 000 nɔ bad O.

Na fɔ kɔl Fudia naw ɛn tɛl

Am bɔt di mɔni.

Kongoma:

Fudia fɔ pe Le300, 000.

Yu no se wi gɛt fɔ pe fɔ mampama.

So we wi ol di mɔni

Naw wi go gi di ɔfisa ɛn wi go

wet de te nɛt kam.

He calls Fudia's phone.

Fudia hɛlo.

Gud yus….

Wi dɔn strayk di dil wit

di ɔfisa….yɛs, yɛs.

Wet, wet

Nɔ gladi yet…di ɔfisa dɛn

de aks fɔ Le500, 000….

Bɔt mi ɛn Kongosa ebul tɔk to dɛm

Fɔ mek dɛm ol Le300, 000….

Yɛs dɛn se dɛn
go ol am.......oke wi de kam
tek di moni rayt naw.
He cuts the phone and gives Kongosa a high five.
As they burst into a song, they dance around each other:
Kongosa ɛn Kongoma
Kongosa ɛn Kongoma
Kongosa ɛn Kongoma
Kongosa ɛn Kongoma
Kongosa ɛn Kongoma
Kongosa ɛn Kongoma
Kongosa en Kongoma
Kongosa ɛn Kongoma
Kongosa ɛn Kongoma

They exit the scene.

THE CURTAINS FALL

ACT THREE
SCENE FOUR

Falilu enters the scene and hesitates as he approaches Khadija's parents' house. He is frustrated from not being able to see Khadija. He paces back and forth and finally picks up courage to confront Khadija's mother who is preparing food outside of her house. Isatu sees Falilu and fears that his appearance at the home means trouble for everyone. Isatu is now displaying fear and making signs to Falilu to go away.

Falilu:

Good morning, Madam.

Mother:

Good morning, young man.

How can I help you?

Falilu:

My name is Falilu.

Mother:

Okay. How can I help you?

Falilu:

I am from the university,

A friend of Khadija's.

Mother:

In shock, she drops the spoon in her hand.

Why are you here?

Falilu:

Khadija is my year mate and I am here...

Mother:

Obstructs instantly.

I know who you are.

What I do not

Know is why you have to continue
To pursue Khadija even after you have
Succeeded in throwing her future
Outside of the university and contributed
In making her the daughter of *Ja'hanama*.

Falilu:

This is not true, Madam.
I am one of Khadija's
Well wishers and always
Want her to succeed in whatever she does.

Mother:

Like luring her into early sex, right?
You have had sex with her
Many many times.
She went to college
A virgin and God-fearing daughter
Of mine...but you...you...you!
You will not let her be. You have
To defile her body and her mind.
If her father was
In the house right now you
Will not continue to stand
There talking to me.

Falilu:

Madam, your daughter did not do
Any such thing.
She is still the same
Girl you sent to the university.

Mother:

Leave! I want you to leave.

> *Falilu continues to stand, speechless.*
> You will not leave?
> You will stand
> There until I die of your wickedness?
> Isatu give me that bucket full of water
> To pour it on this satanic object.

Isatu:

> But aunty maybe you should
> Listen to him.
> He probably has something
> To tell you about cousin Khadija.

Mother:

> *She turns around in fury.*
> Get out of my sight, *Yankamadi Sofah*!
> You will be the next one to bring filth
> Into this house, but I will not have
> Any of that to happen here, *Insha'Allah*!
> *She dashes for the bucket of water and runs to pour it on*
> *Falilu before Falilu swiftly takes to his heels. The scene*
> *changes to an open clearing in the forest. Kongosa, Kongoma*
> *and Njai enter the scene.*

Njai:

> Free! Free! Free at last.
> Thank God almighty
> I am free at last!

Kongosa:

> Yu nɔ fri o!
> Di agrimɛnt wit di ɔfisa dɛm
> Na dat yu de kam si Fudia dɔn
> Yu go bak.

Afta ɔl yu tɛm nɔ
Bɛtɛ egen na jel.
Yu gɛt fɔ bia!

Njai:

He looks around him, ignoring them.
But where is Fudia, my love?

Kongoma:

O! i go de kam jisnɔ.

Njai:

Oh Fudia, my love.
Come to me.
I have not seen you for God
Knows how long.

Kongosa:

Na tru, Fudia fayn o.
Fudia dɔn fayn o.
Yu go lɛk am we yu si am.

Njai:

I know she is a child of God.
She glitters like the stars
Above our heads now.
He spots Fudia entering the scene.
Speaking of the devil....
No, no, no,
Speaking of the angel.
There she comes.

Fudia:

She rushes to hug Njai.
Oh my dearest!
I miss you so so much.

They hug and kiss.

Kongoma:

Kongosa,

Wi yon dɔn dɔn na ya o.

Mek wi de ɛskuz dɛm fɔs ba.

Kongoma:

Nɔ to ple o.

Mek wi go lik mampama ya...

bɔt na yu de pe tide o.

Kongosa:

Na lay na yu fɔ pe.

Mek wi de go fɔs.

They exit the scene.

Njai:

Darling, I missed you so much.

Away from you, I felt like I had

Lost an organ from my body.

Fudia:

My world

Turned upside down

When you were gone from me.

You made me a queen when you

Proposed to me the night

you were taken away.

I still wear the ring.

Shows Njai the ring on her finger.

Njai:

After this is over,

I want to make

You my wife.

I want to hold you
In my arms until kingdom come.

Fudia:

Professor Sankoh told me
That the university has said that you
Will be allowed
To complete your course
When you are set free.
She pauses.
Njai, I give you my word to wait
For you to come from prison.

Njai:

He disengages from Fudia confusedly.
Fudia it's three years more.
I have three years more in prison!

Fudia:

I know and
I am prepared to wait.

Njai:

We cannot have it that way, Fudia.
I don't have any more patience
To do three years.

Fudia:

What does that mean, Njai?

Njai:

Can't you see I'm free now?
Can't you see
I'm here with you?
We can run away from
Here to another country.

Fudia:

Please Njai, lower your voice,
The officers are somewhere listening.
She moves closer and whispers.
How do we
Go about escaping from the country?
Is it not too risky?

Njai:

Risky?
What is the risk?
I am out and free!
He kneels before Fudia and takes her hand.
No, it's not risky. If you have some
Money on you, we can increase the bribe
To the officers to turn the other way.
Or, we can just leave here quietly.

Fudia:

He searches her bag frustratingly.
I don't have any money
Here with me.
I don't.
Oh dear, what shall we do now?

Njai:

Shhhhhhh! Let's go away.
*They attempt to move away from the scene. In that instant,
sporadic gunfire engages from the forest. Bullets pierce Fudia.
She cries aloud and falls. Njai, in fear looks over her for a
brief while but turns and runs away from the scene. Two
officers enter and exit the scene, chasing Njai. Instantly,*

Falilu enters from the other end and spots Fudia on the floor, bleeding.

Falilu:

Fudia! Fudia! Fudia!

Fudia continues to scream for help. Falilu squats on the ground and picks her up.

Fudia:

I'm dying, Falilu, I'm dying.

Falilu:

Don't die on me, please, Fudia.
Don't die on me.
He takes his phone and calls for help.
Who did this to you and
How did it happen?

Fudia:

The police shot me. Njai…
Njai was here.
The police
Have gone after him

Falilu:

Fudia, please hold on
Help is on the way.

Fudia:

Falilu, please take good care
Of my mother for me.
Please look after my family
And care for them.

Falilu:

Don't
Do this to me, Fudia.

Don't.
He kisses Fudia.

Fudia:

She smiles painfully and breathlessly.
You just kissed me.

Falilu:

I should have done this a long ago.
And you are not going to die on me.

Fudia:

In a weak voice
Do it again, please.

Falilu:

Fudiiiiaaaa

Fudia:

Just do it!

Falilu:

Slowly reaches for the lips of Fudia whose head is in his arms and plants a long kiss. After a long while he detaches.
Are you okay now?

Fudia:

You love me, don't you?

Falilu:

You are always beautiful
Inside and outside.

Fudia:

You never once told me until
My dying day.
She sobs.
You should have told me; you should have...
You should have made me

Felt like you cared.
And now I'm dying in the arms
Of someone who should have...

Falilu:

Why do you talk like that?
Why has this little shot
Become a dying matter?
Help is on the way, the ambulance
Will arrive here
Soon and all will be well.

Fudia:

I love you too, Falilu.
I wish I'd had
The guts to let you know
Before I'd gone thinking that—
O, maybe
We were only meant to be family.
She pauses.
Like family friends...

Falilu:

Don't we have to catch
Up on a lot, dear Fudia?
Just get back from this shot
And we will have a lot to chat about.
Suddenly, from the thick of the forest, Khadija emerges. In
shock, she pauses, and then runs over to Falilu and Fudia.

Falilu:

Fudia was shot
By some police officers.
We are waiting for help.

Fudia:

You come at the right time, Khadija.

I never meant to......

Never......

Khadija:

Please don't try to say anything....

*Fudia chokes and spits more blood. Falilu and Khadija
scream and cry.*

Fudia:

Khadija, give me your hand.

Your hand too, Falilu.

*Khadija stretches her hand to Fudia. Falilu too stretches his
hand.*

Khadija please take care of Falilu

and Falilu take care of Khadija.

You are both each other's

To hold and to keep.

*Enter Kongoma and Kongosa followed by Alhaji Majid,
Mother of Khadija and Isatu.*

Alhaji Majid:

What godless act

I see happening here?

Who is the author of this evil deed?

How can you defile

The hand of my daughter?

Mother:

O evil

Why come upon my head?

I am dead in shame.

Utter shame.

Kongoma:

    Alaji a tink se yu ɛn yu wɛf

    Nid fɔ gɛt klia undastandin

    ɔf dis wɔld we wi de so.

    Luk unda Falilu in fut,

    Na pipul pikin

    Ledɔm de, day wan.

    Da pikin we day so go na yu os

    Fɔ tɔk to yu way yu nid fɔ listin

    To yu pkin bɔt udat fɔ mared am.

    Yu fel fɔ listin.

    Naw luk di ɛnd.

Alhaji Majid:

    That is none of my making.

    How could I have ever known

    Her behavior would lead her to her death?

Kongosa:

    Na dat ɛksatli

    Kongoma de talk.

    We una we na perɛnt sɛn

    Pikin dɛn go skul,

    una fɔ ɛkspɛkt se

    Dɛn tinkin go cheng

    Pas una yon dɛm bikɔz ɔf dɛn

    Buk lanin.

    Yu nɔ go ɛva ebul fɔ disayd

    udat i fɔ lɛk ɔ nɔ lɛk.

    Buk de cheng mɔtal man.

    A wish a bin fɔ lan buk.

Mother:

Khadija, as parents, what wrong
Have we done to you that you must
Wish to send us off to our early graves?

Khadija:

Mother you and papa sent
Me to be educated, to be able
To decide for myself.
It has always been my decision
That I wish to get married
To Falilu.
The resolve of my friend
To help honor my decision
Has today caused
Her an early death.
If you two had listened to me
For leaving up
To the education you both
Wanted me to achieve, my friend,
Fudia would be alive today.
She bursts into tears.
Here am I
Watching over the corpse
Of someone's daughter
While I stay alive.
I would serve my conscience best
If I myself should die like her
Instead of continuing in a world
Where what I want
Can never be recognized.

Mother:

> Now, you want to kill the both of us.
> Don't forget that if you kill yourself
> I will follow after.

Isatu:

> Uncle!
> Don't just stand there without doing
> Anything for the two precious women
> In your life, as you have always said.
> Will you afford to lose them because you
> Want to hold on to rusty traditions?

Alhaji Majid:

> *Dropping on his knees, he sobs*
> I love my family
> And I don't want
> Any of them dead.
> *Both Mother and Khadija rush to embrace Alhaji Majid.*

Falilu:

> *He looks at Fudia.*
> Fudia! Fudia!
> O my God,
> How I wish I could have
> Saved you from dying!

Khadija:

> Oh, no! Oh my God.
> Is she dead, are you sure?
> She could not be just dead.
> *Both Falilu and Khadija scream and cry bitterly. Then Njai enters. Falilu rises in anger while the others merely stare.*

Njai:

> *Uncontrollably falls on the corpse of Fudia, sobbing.*
> But for me and the arrogance
> Lurked in me, you wouldn't have lost
> Your precious life.
> The world gave me a space
> To breathe, I gave it a belching hate.
> The world gave me
> An opportunity to learn,
> I chose to kick it in the face.
> The world gave me friends,
> I despised them with a thorny fence
> Between us.
> The world gave me you, Fudia,
> I killed you!

Falilu:

> *Turns to Njai in anger.*
> I swear to God,
> If the world forgives you,
> I will hunt you and kill you
> With my bare hands!
> *Khadija reaches for the back of Falilu to calm him down. At this point, a louder siren of an ambulance is heard approaching. Two police officers enter the scene and handcuff Njai and exit with him. Alhaji Majid wraps his hands around his wife, Khadija and Isatu, as they walk away from the scene. Falilu still holds Fudia in his hands and bowing over her dead body sobbing. The siren continues to blast louder and louder...*

THE CURTAIN FALLS